THE HEALTH AND WEALTH PARADOX

Praise for *The Health and Wealth Paradox*

'A brilliant take on how health and wealth follow the same timeless principles. Simple, practical, inspiring.'
—Jitendra Chouksey,
founder and CEO, FITTR

'This book dives deep into the timeless link between smart investing and healthy eating. If you want to become fitter and wealthier, read it.'
—Brian Feroldi, financial educator and author of
Why Does the Stock Market Go Up?

'I want to compliment Ankush and Mihir for the great execution of what should be an obvious idea, but isn't! That health and wealth are two sides of a coin and must be looked after simultaneously is expertly communicated in the book. I see this helping many families in their money and health journey.'
—Monika Halan, author of *Let's Talk Money,*
Let's Talk Mutual Funds, Let's Talk Legacy

THE HEALTH AND WEALTH PARADOX

HOW TO USE FIRST PRINCIPLES THINKING TO ACHIEVE BOTH

ANKUSH DATAR | MIHIR PATKI

HarperCollins *Publishers* India

First published in India by HarperCollins *Publishers* 2024
4th Floor, Tower A, Building No. 10, DLF Cyber City,
DLF Phase II, Gurugram, Haryana – 122002
www.harpercollins.co.in

2 4 6 8 10 9 7 5 3 1

Copyright © Ankush Datar and Mihir Patki 2024

P-ISBN: 978-93-6569-557-1
E-ISBN: 978-93-6569-150-4

The views and opinions expressed in this book are the authors' own and the facts are as reported by them, and the publishers are not in any way liable for the same.

Ankush Datar and Mihir Patki assert the moral right to be identified as the authors of this work.

All rights reserved. No part of this publication may be reproduced, stored in a retrieval system, or transmitted, in any form or by any means, electronic, mechanical, photocopying, recording or otherwise, without the prior permission of the publishers.

Typeset in 11.5/15.2 Aldine401 BT at
HarperCollins *Publishers* India

Printed and bound at
Thomson Press (India) Ltd

This book is produced from independently certified FSC® paper to ensure responsible forest management.

To the stock markets, for teaching me about emotions such as greed, envy, jealousy, contentment and uncertainty.

To the gym and the roads where I run, for teaching me about delayed gratification, compounding, process and mindset.

To nutritious as well as junk food, for teaching me about balance and what matters most.

To my mother and father, who gave me the privilege to enjoy all this and let me spread my wings.

To my late grandparents, my partner and my family, friends, teachers and colleagues.

I could give a long speech, but these are the experiences and people that have shaped me into the person I am today. This book would not be possible without all of you.

—Ankush Datar

To my wife, Payal, with whom I share the way of life described in this book, and our daughter, Mira, who has just begun to discover the ways of the world.

Also to Pup, who gave us immense joy for three weeks but could not make it to this world.

To my parents for teaching me to live happily below means.

—Mihir Patki

Additional Disclaimer

This book explores the complex and multifaceted topics of fitness and health and their correlation to investing from various perspectives, including the authors' lived experiences, insights of other individuals and allied reflections. It is important to note that the authors are not medical professionals, and that the information provided within these pages is not intended as a substitute for professional medical advice, diagnosis or treatment, and this book does not offer medical guidance. Nothing contained herein may be construed to be a treatment or prescription for any disease or disorder. Concomitantly, the information provided in this book also does not constitute financial, investment or legal advice. Readers are encouraged to seek the guidance of a qualified financial advisor or other professional before making any investment decisions. The authors and publisher are not responsible for any financial outcomes resulting from the use of the information in this book. Neither the authors nor the publisher assume responsibility for any actions taken based on the information presented in this book.

Some names and identifying details have been changed to protect the privacy of individuals. Any liability arising from mistaking characters or events as real is disclaimed by the author and publisher.

None of the views shared by the authors represent the views of their respective employers; they are the authors' independent views.

Contents

Authors' Note   ix

Preface   xv

1. Your Plan Is Your North Star   1
2. Invisible to the Naked Eye   29
3. Less Is More   48
4. The Power of Compounding   74
5. Information Overload   104
6. Don't Judge a Book by Its Cover   125
7. The Pain and Value of Paying   156
8. Twisting the Data   165
9. Reverse Compounding   183
10. Delayed Gratification   198

| 11. | Ancient Wisdom | 214 |
| 12. | Healthy Is Wealthy | 227 |

| *Acknowledgements* | 243 |
| *Notes* | 249 |

Authors' Note

Serendipity—that is the most apt word to describe how this book came into being.

Back in 2020, I (Ankush) started full-time putting out blogs, and wrote an article on long-term investing and fitness—having never imagined it would connect me with my co-author today. The purpose of the article was to simply get fleeting thoughts on similarities between the principles of long-term investing and fitness, which I observed over the years, out of my head.

On 22 July 2021, I stumbled upon a tweet by Mihir's start-up, Multipie, which was conducting a webinar on the parallels between investing and nutrition.

Multipie ✓
@MultipieSocial

The power of compounding & incremental change applies to both investing and nutrition. Join our co-founder @mihir_patki, as he explores these two inter-connected worlds.

When: 11:00 - 12:00 PM I Sunday 25th July 2021
Register: bit.ly/36RxN7u
Via: edgecommunity.org

I registered for it right away. I would probably be one of the few attending the workshop live on a Sunday morning, because I felt this topic would be right up my alley and I would be able to engage in a meaningful way.

Before the session, Mihir tweeted the registration link of the workshop on 24 July 2021, and I replied to him with a link to my blog post.

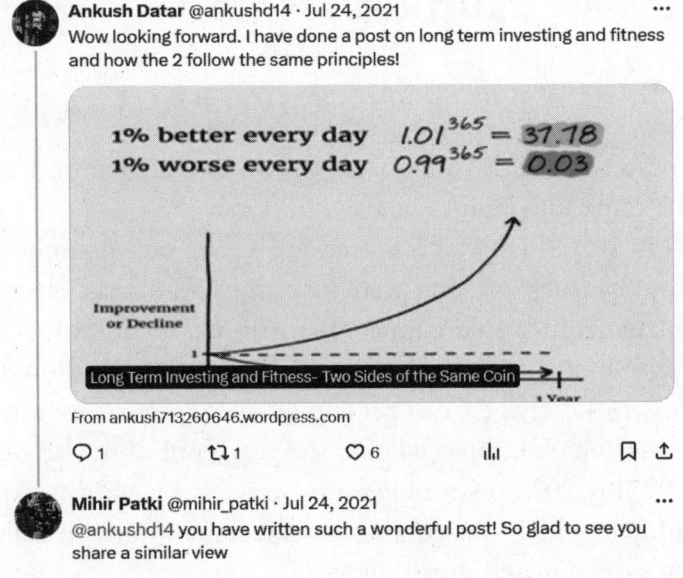

I was surprised to receive a response from Mihir, appreciating the post. Two strangers sharing similar views were thus connected via the internet.

We continued to have conversations here and there on the same platform, mainly exchanging in nonsensical banter or stoic wisdom—on X (formerly Twitter), there's a very thin line between the two.

Then, in 2022, the equity markets went into correction mode after a stellar run since 2020. This is the time when investors usually get a little jittery, wondering whether it's

Authors' Note

a good time to pull out money from the markets or not. My friend Abhijeet Salelkar was in that same dilemma, and called me one evening post a bloodbath correction to discuss what the next step should be.

He told me his investor friend was sitting with him, and suggested I come down to discuss the markets and the portfolio. I was hoping it wouldn't be another doomsday prophet or naysayer. To my surprise, it was Mihir. So, we met in person for the first time and exchanged numbers.

Within a few months, Mihir messaged me asking if I wanted to write a book with him. It took me just five minutes to respond that I was open to the idea, and I suggested we meet to discuss. The idea of writing a book had been somewhere in my subconscious, but it wasn't something I thought of pursuing actively.

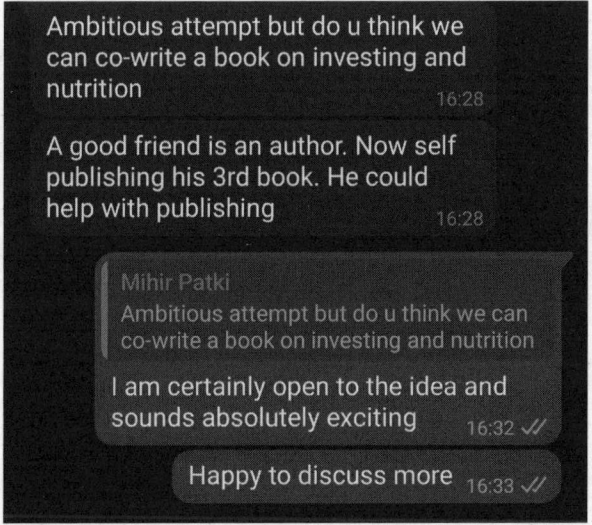

Mihir and I met at his office, and there was an instant connection regarding the ideas and chapters of the book. It took us just one meeting to conclude this idea deserved a book.

This is where our old friend Serendipity came to the fore again, this time in the form of Shreya Punj, to whom we are extremely grateful. I had previously interacted with Shreya when she was a part-time editor with *Truth Be Told*, the health and fitness newsletter, to which I had contributed numerous articles.

Shreya had been working as a consultant for up-and-coming writers, helping them approach publishing houses and preparing a structured way to pitch book ideas. She played a crucial role in helping us prepare the pitch deck to communicate the idea to publishers. She never takes enough credit for the help she provides.

Through her, we connected with Sachin Sharma, a senior publisher at HarperCollins. Fortunately, Sachin believed in the concept of health and wealth and saw the glaring similarities between the two topics. Sachin was well-acquainted with the investing part of the book, having worked with best-selling authors like Gautam Baid and Monika Halan, which made it easy for us to explain our idea.

After our initial talks, it took a few months for us to hear back, but the most amazing moment was receiving the call from Sachin confirming that the book was going through. This gave us enough confidence to aggressively start preparing the book.

How to Read This Book

We have written this volume to serve as a mental model on first principles thinking, rather than conventional concepts which you can easily search on the internet or read in a text book. It is more of 'what works and what has worked over the years' rather than what you should do.

Ideally, you should peruse it in the chronological order of chapters, as we would like to ingrain certain principles in your mind before you go on to subsequent chapters.

As stated in the preface, we have documented lessons from the history of business, health, psychology, investing and more such topics, and most importantly, from our shared personal experiences—we have consistently and rigorously applied these principles to our lives in our own unique ways, coming from different backgrounds and circumstances. It is our belief that the perspectives can be applied to individuals across various age groups and situations.

These timeless principles, which have lived on for centuries, will continue to do so in new avatars as humanity progresses.

Note: We have elucidated the concepts in this book through tables and figures. However, given the print-layout limitations and for clarity, please refer to them on the sources mentioned.

The detailed notes pertaining to this book are available on the HarperCollins *Publishers* India website. Scan this QR code to access the same.

Preface

Mr Agarwal is one of the most successful investors in the world. A workaholic, he has delivered stellar returns to his investors while also helping build companies from the ground up.

He is worth $100 million today. Society looks up to him as a role model. But what about Mr Agarwal himself? How does he feel?

Over the years, he has primarily focussed on work. By age forty, he has become obese, looks well beyond his age and is physically incapable of spending quality time with his young kids and family, which is what he worked so hard for.

He recently suffered a 'sudden' heart attack due to the long hours he dedicated to work.

'Sudden' is largely a myth. Most things that happen suddenly are the result of years and years of bad habits. Now, what is the use of Mr Agarwal's $100-million net worth if he is not in a condition to spend time with his loved ones?

Unlike money or net worth, the metrics of health don't magically pop up on a screen, but the scoreboard is always ticking.

What if he had read the labels of the food he was eating as diligently as he evaluated the financial statements of companies? What if he had applied the same principle 'working hard today for a better tomorrow' to his health? Was all this worth it if he could not enjoy the fruits of his labour with the people around him?

Just like Mr Agarwal, there have been millions of people who believe this as a necessary trade-off. Seeing the success of such individuals, millions of others follow suit and preach only this one true method—the chase for wealth implies a proportionate loss in health. This eventually becomes the benchmark for society.

Now, let's turn the situation around, and imagine that Mr Agarwal is a company founder with borderline health issues, who is approaching an investor for funds. Would this investor not consider Mr Agarwal's health issues a potential risk for investing in the business?

In the last few decades, many individuals with corporate success have started posing questions about the toll this method has taken on their health. They have publicly shared certain regrets about their paths. But most people still refuse to acknowledge this because from a young age—they have been conditioned to think a certain way.

What if we told you, this is nothing but an age-old myth that has not been questioned enough? What if you can work as hard as you want and still be healthy? What if doing so makes you a better investor and human being, as well as a more productive person in general?

Take a moment and ask yourself why you didn't think this was possible. It is probably because you looked at Mr Agarwal as the example.

Almost everyone decides to abandon common sense about health once they begin their journey towards creating wealth.

Investing is known as an interdisciplinary practice, but we would say, so is health. In fact, the principles of health and wealth are so deeply intertwined that one can learn from either discipline and apply the lessons across both.

Long-term investing follows principles such as delayed gratification, the power of compounding and not judging a book by its cover.

But have you ever wondered how these same principles can be applied to your health? Or that the principles of being healthy can help you create wealth?

'Health is wealth' is not just an old cliché, and this book explains why. The principles have been hiding in plain sight within the wisdom we have received from our ancestors, but most of us have conveniently overlooked them.

Are you the person rushing to catch a flight at the airport, glancing through this book to see what valuable insights you may obtain? To catch your attention, we want to mention how skipping that meal on your flight is going to benefit you greatly, and how spending money on this book rather than on that java-chip drink is a wise investment.

Just because some hustler said you need to sacrifice health for wealth, did you not pause and reflect that there could be an alternative?

We want to take you on a journey through that alternative scenario. The following pages contain various concepts, stories from ancient wisdom, as well as transformations from our own lives and experiences.

If you are looking for a magic pill to become fit, or stock picks that will go 100x, this is not the book for you. But it does contain a path to that destination. There won't be any false promises; only cold, hard truths.

Unlike certain fitfluencers and finfluencers who promise you 'five ways to get rich and healthy', there are no hacks here. The book also aims to break down the psychology of why these types of influencers thrive in today's society.

If you are an investing expert, you may cringe at certain concepts. If you are a nutrition expert or a doctor, you may not agree with certain things we have to say. We are not asking the reader to do as we did; instead, we are saying, 'we have done this and it has worked extremely well for us', as it has for many others too.

A human being is always chasing health or wealth, or even both, at some point in their life, so why not be acquainted with the most important principles linking the two together?

This book is also a consolidation of wisdom from various practitioners from the world of investing, business, health and wellness, who have shared and documented their learnings and life experiences. Without their insights, we may not have learned much or applied these principles to our lives, let alone written a book about them.

Well beyond investing and fitness, there are discussions on health, envy, greed, ancient wisdom, delayed gratification and traditional psychological measures that tie health and wealth together. There are also chapters that aim to empower the youth with certain concepts they can learn at an early stage and apply once they step into the real world; concepts we wished we had had access to at the same point in our lives.

1

Your Plan Is Your North Star

> When you first study a field, it seems like you have to memorize a zillion things. You don't. What you need is to identify the three-to-five core principles that govern the field. The million things you thought you had to memorize are various combinations of the core principles.
>
> **John Reed**[1]

The concepts of health and wealth follow a similar form of first principles thinking. It begins by defining an allocation plan based on what we want to achieve.

This chapter aims to provide a blueprint and a heuristic roadmap of first principles thinking rather than advising on a particular plan, as each person's plan would be subjective to their unique preferences and objectives. This is more about the basic set of actions you can take to kickstart your knowledge journey.

Consider the following questions. How do fit individuals change their body shapes and weights at will? How do ace investors always appear calm?

It's simple: they follow a plan.

Of course, this is the most boring answer to these questions. Even we cringed a little typing out these words, but it is the brutal truth. There aren't going to be any flashy answers to provide an engagement-worthy tweet.

As simple as it sounds, almost all successful individuals across various fields essentially do two things:

1. Make a plan.
2. Stick to it.

The hard part is step 2—sticking to the plan. I am sure that even the most successful professionals in their fields, just like all other human beings, came to this realization through trial and error.

When it comes to our health, most of us go through this vicious cycle:

1. We start a diet that works for a while, until it doesn't anymore.
2. We don't think it will be sustainable, so we switch to the next in-vogue diet, because a friend transformed themselves.
3. We try this new diet very meticulously for a week, then skip a day, thinking, 'It's the weekend. I'll resume from Monday.' Before we know it, the 'weekend' turns into forever, and we are left searching for another quick-fix diet.

Meanwhile, in the investing world:

1. We invest in a mutual fund or buy a stock on a hot tip. It works until it doesn't.

2. We switch to another fund or stock because someone peddles a story—an ace investor is buying that stock so it must surely go up. Or maybe we end up going for a fund that has had a phenomenal past run, as against the fund we are invested in.

This cycle never ends.

Monika Halan, in her book *Let's Talk Mutual Funds*, says, 'The earlier you have a first-principles-based mental roadmap, the better your money will serve you.'[2]

There are broadly three mental maps that one can keep handy when it comes to health and wealth:
1. Allocate between macronutrients and asset allocation as per your profile.
2. Pick the right elements within the above two.
3. Keep following steps 1 and 2 consistently over a long time, with intermittent reviews.

Let's dive deep into the basic principles of these mental maps.

First Principles of Nutrition

These are very basic parameters we wish were taught at an early age. But, as with almost all human beings, we were forced to learn them due to circumstances.

Nutrients come in two broad categories—macronutrients and micronutrients.

Macronutrients consist of carbohydrates, proteins and fats, known together as 'CPF'.

Micronutrients, meanwhile, consist of vitamins and minerals, which are essential for the overall health and well-being of the body. They are taken in relatively small quantities but play crucial roles in various physiological functions—for example, vitamins A, B-complex, C, D, E and K are necessary for functions such as vision, immune support, energy metabolism and bone health.

Micronutrients are typically obtained from within macronutrients, or through supplementation when food is not doing the job.

We will cover the basic principles of macronutrients. Micronutrients usually fall in place if you are getting your macronutrients from natural sources.

Carbohydrates

Think of these as the main fuel-storage source of the body. If we are going for a long run or intense exercise and activity, you will need to fuel the tank accordingly for that particular activity—be it a long-distance run or a heavy workout, or to refuel a depleted tank.

Proteins

These are the building blocks of our body and are arguably the most important piece in the macronutrient puzzle. They are vital for strengthening our bones, organs, hormones, enzymes and more. They even have a secondary role of acting as energy storage for the proverbial 'rainy day'.

Fats

These are the most important store of energy in our bodies, and no, they don't make us 'fat'. Dietary fat is different from body fat. They serve as transport mechanisms for vital nutrients across the body, and are also responsible for regular hormonal functions.

What Are Calories?

A calorie is a measure of the energy content of food. In scientific terms, it is defined as the amount of heat required to raise the temperature of one kilogram of water by one degree Celsius.

Every gram of carbohydrate contains 4 calories; every gram of protein contains 4 calories, and every gram of fat contains 9 calories.

So, how many calories should one consume and what is the best allocation between CPF? This can be broken down in simple terms, but let us first understand some basic terminology.

Basal Metabolic Rate (BMR)

This is the minimum amount of energy required to sustain the basic physiological functions of the body, including breathing, circulation, maintaining body temperature, and other metabolic processes. The BMR represents the energy the body consumes at rest, in a post-absorptive state (when a person has not eaten for at least 12 hours), and in a thermoneutral environment (comfortable room temperature). It accounts for approximately 60–70 per cent of the total energy expenditure of an individual. The BMR can vary based on factors such as age, gender, body composition and genetics. Generally, larger individuals and those with more muscle mass (not just large body fat) have higher BMRs than smaller individuals with less muscle mass.

Knowing one's BMR can be useful in determining the daily caloric needs required to maintain, gain or lose weight.

Thermic Effect of Food (TEF)

Every food in the CPF categories uses energy to be digested. The TEF is the number of calories the body burns in digesting and absorbing nutrients from food. The body uses the most energy to break down proteins. Dietary fats also require more energy to digest. Carbohydrates are easily digested and require less energy to process, making them less satiating compared to the same quantities of protein and fat.

However, we know by now that each macronutrient has its place. This is one of the key reasons why 'protein-rich diet' is a term we often hear in the context of people trying to lose weight.

Non-exercise-Activity-Thermogenesis (NEAT)

This is the movement of the body in non-exercise form. It is part of the calories we burn outside our actual workout.

Those 10,000 steps of walking, going to the washroom, going to the kitchen to grab a meal—all these activities burn calories too, and are as important in active calories burnt as the next component, EAT.

Exercise-Activity Thermogenesis (EAT)

These are the number of active calories we burn during a workout.

Activity	Calories burnt in 1 hour of activity
Strength training	606 calories at a moderate pace
Walking	224 calories for a person weighing 70 kg
Running	314 calories at a moderate pace

These are broad numbers; calories burnt could vary based on metabolism and other factors. The intensity of the workout could also cause fluctuations in calorie burn.

However, this does not imply that one should pursue activities solely based on their calorie-burning potential. Strength training is arguably the most important activity. We will delve deeper into this in a later chapter, and generally express our preference for it.

Basic Formulae for Calorie Counting

The sum of BMR, TEF, NEAT and EAT is the Total Energy Expended (TEE), the number of calories your body burns through your BMR combined with the activities that you do.

$$TEE = BMR + NEAT + EAT + TEF$$

Now that we have defined the basic ingredients, let's move on to some simple mathematical equations. By inputting one's height and weight into a basic BMR and TEE calculator, which one can easily find through an internet search, one can compute these two figures.

So, how many calories should one consume? This brings us to Equation 1: how many calories should one consume?

Equation 1:

$$BMR < 4C + 4P + 9F < TEE$$

Simple maths:

Fewer calories consumed = weight loss

Too less calories (below BMR) = immunity loss

$$4C + 4P + 9F < TEE$$

which entails being in a caloric deficit, entailing weight loss.

$$4C + 4P + 9F = TEE$$

which entails being in a caloric maintenance, entailing weight maintenance.

$$4C + 4P + 9F > TEE$$

which entails being in a caloric surplus, entailing weight gain.

The hardest part is to maintain those calories and thus our health, similar to how it is harder to maintain wealth than to earn it.

Now our goal isn't mere weight loss—this could occur due to loss of fat (good) as well as loss of muscle (bad).

The goal of a plan should be fat loss and/or gaining muscles and that is the efficient application of these equations. To prevent weight loss attributed to muscle loss, one needs to consume an adequate quantity of protein coupled with a decent mix of strength training.

Now, how much protein is adequate? There's no right or wrong answer here. The body needs a minimum of 0.8 grams of protein per kg of body weight for basic human functioning.[3]

Now, keeping this bare minimum in mind, we must also remember that the CPF allocation will differ based on levels of activity. For example, an athlete may have to derive a large part of their calories from C, but also maintain adequate P and F in their macronutrient balance. A corporate employee doing a desk job has absolutely no reason to derive a large part of their calories from C due to the lack of movement and activity. Meanwhile, a diabetic individual may have to reduce calories from C to avoid any sensitivity in their blood glucose.

If one is suffering from a disease, a nutritionist can help with the finer aspects of what to include within this allocation based on one's hormonal health and various other factors, but the idea is that one must empower themselves with these basics of nutrition.

Understanding basic caloric composition and counting is a life skill.

Equation 2:

$$4C:4P:9F = 25:25:50$$

What are the right elements within those macros?

Here, 25:25:50 is the thumb rule that one can start with and then move the equation around based on their lifestyle and circumstance:

- If muscle-building is a priority, then the P element has to be raised from the baseline.

- If fuelling for an event is the priority, then the C element has to be raised from the baseline.
- If one has a genetic predisposition or health issue, then the F element could be tweaked up or down based on the individual's condition.

One must have a broad understanding of the basic formula and tweak it as per their preference.

Does your BMR and TEE change over time? It is said that TEE changes over time with age and metabolism, but some conflicting views say TEE does not reduce.[4]

There are various apps available on the internet that allow us to calculate our macronutrient requirements as well as our calorie counts.

Our Own Goals and Plans

We manually compute our BMR and TEE using a basic calculator on the internet. Calories and CPF split of various food items are easily found online or on food labels.

Mihir's Goal

Maintaining a caloric deficit to lose some weight, coupled with resistance training to maintain muscle. Once weight loss is achieved, stay at maintenance calories.

Height: 5'9"
Weight: 80 kg
BMR: 1,500
TEE: 1,800
Calorie intake: 1,635

Objective: Sustained 165 calorie deficit for three months, with protein and fat given much higher weightage. Total calories are calculated as 4P + 4C + 9F.

Mihir's Plan

Particulars	Quantity	Carbs	Proteins	Fats	Total calories
Breakfast					
Black coffee/tea	1 cup	-	-	-	-
Whole eggs	3	-	18.0 g	15.0 g	207
Butter/ghee/oil	5 g	-	-	5.0 g	45
Cheese	1 cube	0.4 g	5.0 g	7.0 g	85
Breakfast total	-	**0.4 g**	**23.0 g**	**27.0 g**	**337**
Lunch					
Chapatis	2	30.0 g	6.0 g	1.6 g	158
Vegetables	1 cup	14.0 g	4.0 g	2.0 g	90
Dal	1 bowl	29.0 g	11.0 g	5.0 g	205
Lunch total	-	**73.0 g**	**21.0 g**	**8.6 g**	**453.4**
Evening snack					
Black coffee/tea	1 cup	-	-	-	-
Peanuts	25 g	4.0 g	6.5 g	12.5 g	155
Cheese	1 slice	0.4 g	8.0 g	10.0 g	124
Evening snack total	-	**4.4 g**	**14.5 g**	**22.5 g**	**278.1**
Dinner					
Chicken breast	250 g	1.00 g	19.0 g	27.0 g	323
Bhakri	1	-	-	5.0 g	45

Particulars	Quantity	Carbs	Proteins	Fats	Total calories
Oil	1 tsp	38.5 g	3.3 g	-	167
Lettuce	1 cup	-	-	-	-
Tomatoes	50 g	negligible			
Salad dressing	20 g	9.0 g	0.2 g	0.2 g	39
Dinner total	-	**48.5 g**	**22.5 g**	**32.2 g**	**574**
Grand total	-	**126.3 g**	**81 g**	**90.3 g**	**1,642**
Target (g)	-	120 g	105 g	75 g	1,635

Minor differences between actual vs target will always remain. Consistency over perfection is the key here.

Ankush's Goal

Eating at caloric surplus while trying to put on weight, coupled with resistance training and higher-than-baseline protein intake. Once weight gain is achieved, stay at maintenance calories.

Height: 6'0"
Weight: 78 kg
BMR: 1,600
TEE: 2,150
Calorie intake: 2,300

Objective: Sustained 150 calorie surplus for four months with protein and fat in decent quantities and also carbohydrates given sizeable weightage.

Ankush's Plan

Particulars	Quantity	Carbs	Proteins	Fats	Total calories
Breakfast					
Black coffee/tea	1 cup	-	-	-	-
Whole eggs	4	-	24.0 g	20.0 g	296
Groundnut oil	2 tsp	-	-	9.0 g	81
Dahi	200 g	9.4 g	7.0 g	6.6 g	125
Dosa	2	52.0 g	11.0 g	5.0 g	297
Breakfast total	-	**61.4 g**	**42.0 g**	**40.0 g**	**799**
Lunch					
Cucumber and tomatoes	1 cup	negligible			
Groundnut oil	2 tsp	-	-	9.0 g	81
Boneless chicken	200 g	0.6 g	51 g	2.6 g	230
Dal	1 bowl	29.0 g	11.0 g	5.0 g	205
Lunch total	-	**29.6 g**	**62.0 g**	**16.6 g**	**516**
Evening snack					
Black coffee/tea	1 cup	-	-	-	-
Protein bar	1	21.3 g	15.0 g	11.0 g	245
Evening snack total	-	**21.3 g**	**15.0 g**	**11.0 g**	**245**

Particulars	Quantity	Carbs	Proteins	Fats	Total calories
Dinner					
Dahi	200 g	9.4 g	7.0 g	6.6 g	125
Red bell pepper (chopped)	2 cups	18.0 g	0.2 g	3.0 g	100
Whey protein	1 scoop	3.0 g	24.0 g	1.0 g	117
Methi paratha	2	50.0 g	14.0 g	16.0 g	400
Dinner total	-	80.4 g	45.5 g	26.6 g	878
Grand total	-	197.3 g	164.5 g	85.2 g	2,302
Target (g)	-	200.0 g	150 g	100 g	2,300

One of the key points to note here is that we are using a sustained caloric deficit/maintenance for the following reasons:
- To avoid impacting our immunity or metabolism for the sake of achieving a goal.
- To allow us to keep our sanity through the process.
- To build mental discipline through the application of a plan, and understand that it is a lifelong process.

Note how Ankush's plan is a high-carb plan compared to Mihir's due to former's higher level of activity. The carbs and fats part can be played around with based on an individual's blood markers, but protein largely remains constant.

We can now use a similar heuristic roadmap on the first principles of investing. Like nutrition is customized by changing the allocation of macronutrients in one's diet, a financial plan is also customized with three core ingredients.

First Principles of Investing

What Are Asset Classes?

In traditional finance, three asset classes form a part of an individual's portfolio:

Equity: Responsible for growth

Debt: Responsible for protection

Gold: Responsible for diversification or hedging

A fourth asset class is real estate, but we are keeping it out from our allocation for practical purposes—for one, it is illiquid, and two, it involves large indivisible investments. For most people, equity, debt and gold are more than sufficient.

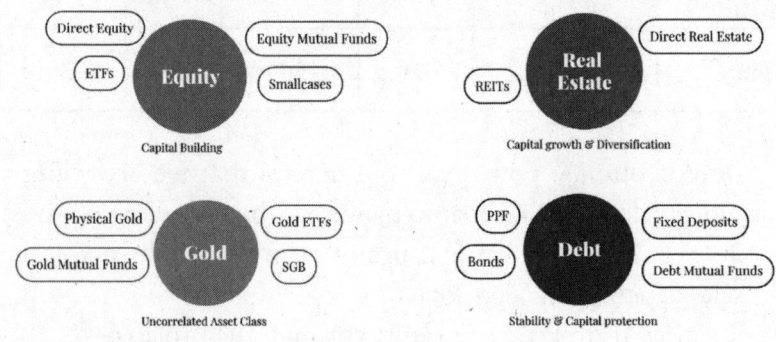

Source: Multipie[5]

Equity investments, such as ownership in companies (stocks, equity mutual funds, ETFs), generally provide higher returns, but come with increased volatility. Cash-flow streams are uncertain and differ in amount and frequency. Underlying stock prices also fluctuate—some more violently than others—which can result in capital losses as well. Equity can be thought of as protein: specifically catered to grow your portfolio, and forming arguably the most key component of your plan.

Debt investments, such as fixed deposits, bonds, debentures and debt mutual funds, generally offer stable returns with lower risk. They provide a fixed (or near-fixed) stream of cash flows followed by the return of capital. Debt can be thought of as fat, bringing balance and stability to the portfolio and ensuring we have a stable, functioning life.

Gold is an asset class that is uncorrelated with equities, thus adding diversification to the portfolio. This does not mean gold should be thought of as carbohydrates—we are not going to squeeze definitions in for the sake of it. We learned that carbohydrates can be selectively consumed the same way gold can be selectively allocated in a portfolio.

CPF in a nutrition plan is equivalent to DEG in an investment plan—in other words, allocation.

The quality of the inputs one puts into each plan is crucial, rather than simply focussing on filling up the CFP and DEG allocation for the sake of it.

What Is Asset Allocation?

Now that we have defined the various ingredients of the financial 'diet', we need to know how to proportion these ingredients into one big pot—our plan. This involves a process called asset allocation.

It is the process of dividing an investment portfolio among different asset classes, such as DEG. The goal is to create a diversified portfolio that can help investors achieve their objectives while minimizing the impact of any one asset class on their overall portfolio performance. By diversifying their investments across different asset classes, investors can potentially reduce their overall risk and increase the potential for long-term returns.

You might ask, 'what is my ideal asset allocation?' Like your nutrition plan, it is unique to the individual and is derived from the person's risk profile. It starts with asking the right questions and answering them truthfully.

There are a couple of basic questions to answer, whether one decides to work themselves or with an investment adviser:
- What are my long-term goals with my money?
- How much money do I need to save for a rainy day?
- Do I have any specific goals?
- Am I adequately covered for a rainy day?

A common misconception is to 'invest more in equity when one is young, and more in debt as one gets older'. The formula of allocation towards equity as 100 minus one's age is archaic and may not apply to the dynamic world we live in today.

A young person wanting to save up for higher education in the near term cannot afford to have too much allocation towards volatile investments such as equity. However a parent who is planning to send their child for higher education in the distant future, can have high allocation to equity.

A person close to retirement may have enough capital to pass on to the next generation after achieving their financial goals, so why shouldn't they invest more in equities to earn a potentially higher return? Does Warren Buffet, at ninety years of age, have 10 per cent of his wealth in equity and 90 per cent in debt?

That is the beauty of asset allocation—it is highly personalized.

Here are a few of the factors that should determine your risk profile:
1. How far out are your future financial goals, in terms of quantum as well as time horizon? The further away they are, the more allocation to equity.
2. What is your emotional quotient? Can you enjoy a good night's sleep without worrying about what happens to

your portfolio value when you wake up? Being at peace is an important factor in investing.
3. What is your time spent on analysing and researching investments? The more time you spend, the higher your conviction, and generally, the higher your risk-taking ability. But this is not a sure-shot recipe for success by any means.

It is important to understand that risk profiles can only be estimated. Moreover, risk profiles change with time as our situation in life changes—the same way the macronutrient split in our nutrition plan may change over time due to health.

Risk profile can be estimated through a set of questions that address the aforementioned three points. Here is an oversimplified way of estimating your risk profile.

Factor	Tending towards Aggressive	Tending towards Conservative
Future financial goals	Largely achieved	Just beginning
Emotional quotient	Can tolerate drawdowns. In other words, a huge fall in the markets makes you go shopping for stocks without worrying about loss of value of existing portfolio.	Can't tolerate large fluctuations in value of portfolio.
Time spent analysing and researching investments	Loves doing this	Ugh, who is going to go through all those numbers?

This table is only a guide and a closer introspection by you or your financial adviser would help. For example, there could be categories such as moderately aggressive and moderately conservative too, which would be subjective.

A better way to quickly understand your risk profile is to judge your past behaviour and see how you reacted to any sudden movements in the market, and ask yourself what the learnings are.

Your risk profile should determine your asset allocation. Here's a short table.

Risk Profile	Allocation towards Debt	Allocation towards Equity
Tending towards aggressive	Less	More
Tending towards conservative	More	Less

How much more or less would be subjective for each individual.

Equity is associated with the term 'aggressive' because it is more volatile but can yield higher returns. Debt, on the other hand, generally provides predictable returns, so it is less volatile but may earn less than equity.

With equity, volatility is the price we pay in the short term to obtain higher returns in the long term.

However, we must point out that internal factors such as risk profile, time horizon and emotional quotient are not the only determinants of asset allocation. Market factors such as valuations and earnings also matter. However, that's a topic for a later chapter. Here, we'll talk about the first principles of asset allocation.

Imagine a scenario in which your risk profile is super aggressive, and say, you want to do a D:E:G allocation of 10:85:5. The market is at an all-time high (not just absolute index value but also in terms of price-to-earnings multiple). Do you think it is prudent to immediately go heavy on equity? Certainly not. External factors are as important as internal factors. So what one does in this case is begin with a slightly lower equity allocation (say, 65–70 per cent) and gradually move to 85 per cent over time.

Markets move through manic and depressive stages. So, if you started with an allocation of, say, 30:65:5 (DEG), and the markets rallied, your allocation might automatically shift to, say, 15:80:5 (DEG) because debt grows gradually while equity surges, especially in bull markets. For such large changes, all you need to do is rebalance your allocation back to 30:65:5, i.e., sell equity and move that money to debt. Conversely, if markets fall, you sell debt and move that money to equity. Done over a long period of time and for significant changes (don't rebalance for minor fluctuations), you will find yourself 'buying low and selling high' automatically.

Now, we come to two concepts we learned about in our financial textbooks:

Systematic risks, which are completely out of our control, such as war, who the next prime minister is going to be, what the federal government is going to do, etc. It is surprising to see how many investors focus on these risks, which they have no control over.

Unsystematic risks, which can be reduced, such as choosing a conservative or aggressive fund, or increasing time horizon.

It's a similar case for health too.

Systematic risks include height, age, genetics and upbringing.

Unsystematic risks include macronutrient split, level of activity and positive thoughts.

The simplest approach for a lay person to choose intrustments within DEG is to have an index fund for equity allocation, high-grade bonds for debt and ETFs for gold.

If one is an astute investor or a researcher, they can pick an active mutual fund or stocks. However, generally, this process is best done under the guidance of an adviser.

Source: Brian Feroldi[6]

How We Allocate Our Own Assets

Mihir's Plan

Wealth creation is the focus, with liquidity being provided via fixed coupons from debt.

Equity	Debt	Gold
60 per cent	36 per cent	4 per cent
A mix of active and passive mutual funds and stocks.	Mix of FDs, debt MFs, bonds for liquidity, stable income and big-ticket equity purchases if markets fall.	As a hedge and for diversification; through sovereign gold bonds.

Ankush's Plan

Wealth creation is the focus, with no big obligations for liquidity to be provided for family.

Equity	Debt	Gold
90 per cent	5 per cent	5 per cent
A mix of stocks, active and passive mutual funds.	Liquid funds for any planned big-ticket purchases	As a hedge and for diversification; through gold ETFs.

Occasional deviations from the plan are absolutely fine, and are in fact required to get you to enjoy the process. One could say, deviations are part of the plan.

In an interesting article for *Business Standard*, financial adviser Harsh Roongta highlighted how he started lifestyle modifications, such as putting a stop to snacking between meals, changing his diet and focussing on sleep and exercise.[7] He also gave up refined foods such as sugar and maida, but allowed himself some leeway to cheat with a sweet indulgence on occasion. By wearing a continuous glucose monitor (CGM), he learned about the impact of sugar. Now, this indulgence is going to keep him sane in his quest for long-term health.

He follows a similar process with his clients by using the concept of a 'mad money' fund for his wealthy investors. The point of a mad money fund is to keep a portion of the proceeds in a fund, where the clients can afford to lose that much money and still not have their financial goals affected. However, with certain exceptions, Roongta also plans in such a way that even if clients do not have enough capital to put into the mad money fund, he tries to allow them to indulge in such an activity.

Careful indulgence will be the key to long-term success, he says.

What's happening here is that a small and infrequent room is being created for indulgences—cheat days for nutrition and high-risk bets in low amounts for the thrill in investing. The key lies in the words 'small' and 'infrequent'.

Not All Calories Are Equal. Nor Are All Investments Same

Management guru Peter Drucker once said, 'Efficiency is doing things right; effectiveness is doing the right things.'[8]

In investing, effectiveness refers to picking the right stocks or instruments, and efficiency refers to appropriate allocation. In nutrition, effectiveness refers to picking the right food, and efficiency refers, again, to appropriate allocation.

The composition or weightage of CPF and DEG matters a lot.

~

Let's go back in time to December 2007. From March 2002 to December 2007, equities gave a 443 per cent return, while debt returns were modest at 39 per cent. In December 2007, all being hunky-dory, one would have been tempted to make an equity-heavy allocation. After all, seeing elevated markets and high returns for such a long time makes one believe that their portfolio is invincible.

But from January 2008 to March 2013, equities returned negative 7 per cent and debt returned a handsome 41 per cent.

The ideal portfolio would have started off with a balanced allocation, then reduced allocation towards equity as the markets rose towards the end of 2007, and then would have been protected to a great extent for the next five years with a higher allocation in debt.

But it would also depend on your investment horizon—an investor who had a long horizon and no need of liquidity would not have been as heavily impacted with an investment in equity as an investor who had a target goal set for 2010.

Let us apply the 2008 scenario to our own portfolios—Ankush's would have taken a bigger beating than Mihir's, but neither would be too panicked by this, as the asset allocation plan was set with a very long-term objective in mind, and this would be part and parcel of that journey.

Nobody knows how the market is going to perform, but you can use asset allocation to increase your probability of growing your portfolio in a certain way while absorbing shocks.

Here's how equities, debt and gold have performed over the last two decades. Equities have returned the highest figures, but observe the ups and downs. Debt is relatively stable with moderate returns. Gold is the most stable with the lowest returns.

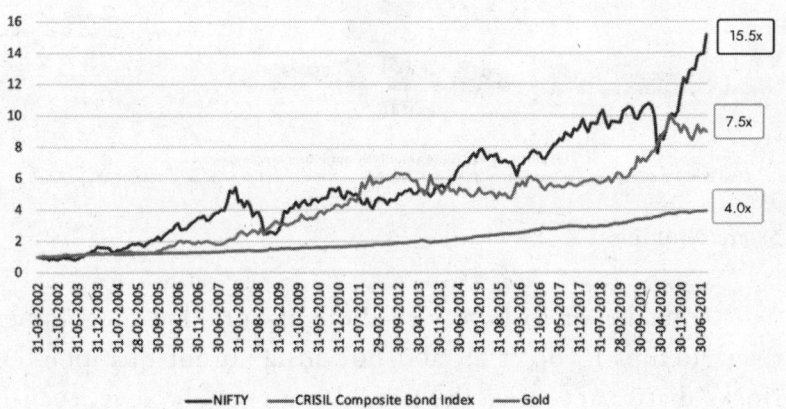

Data up to 30 June 2021

Source: NSE India, CRISIL.

Gold, equity and debt have rallied since then—by the time we are writing in 2024, the gap between the returns from gold and equity have narrowed. These asset-class fluctuations will keep happening with changes in the macroeconomic landscape.

Equities are volatile and have a magnifying effect. Debt is relatively stable and offers capital protection to some extent.

It is not enough to merely create savings. Poorly allocated savings are equivalent to playing Jenga with your portfolio. Here's what it would look like—threatening to collapse, but somehow held back by some prudent investments.

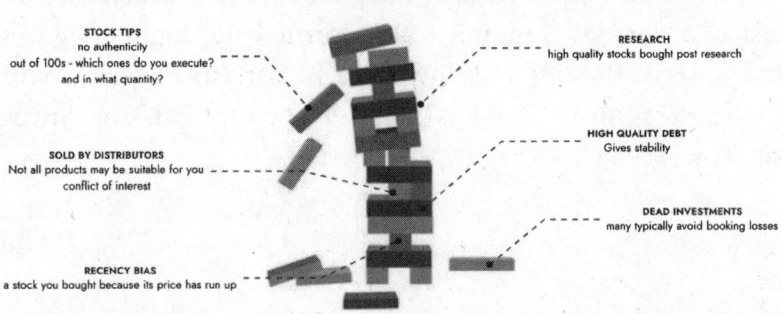

Poorly structured portfolio = stress, lower returns

It is difficult to create wealth through one single stock
Even if one manages to get lucky, it is difficult to sustain and grow wealth without a structured approach

Source: Multipie[9]

It is far better to have well-thought-out allocations rather than attempt to do it all and buy insignificant quantities of stocks that won't move the needle at a portfolio level even if they increase by 100x.

Conversely, having outsized allocations negatively impacts the portfolio even with small downward movements in the underlying assets.

You are not here to take bets on future prices of assets; you are here to allocate over a long period of time into the asset classes that could probably grow the fastest.

Many people can identify a winning stock or fund, but what differentiates the good from the great is the position sizing of that stock. Given that the average success rate for an investor is typically less than 50 per cent, it matters where this money is being put to use. It is not just the frequency of winning that matters, but also the frequency multiplied by the magnitude of the payoff, referred to by Michael Mauboussin as the 'Babe Ruth effect'.[10] The only way an average Joe like us can get a multiplier effect without taking outsized risks is by following asset allocation over a long period of time.

The same holds true for allocation within asset classes. Not all stocks you buy will outperform; some might. Every instrument—whether stock, mutual fund, PMS or AIF—comes with its own set of pluses and minuses. Hence, allocate and rebalance as per your risk profile. Your allocation across DEG, as well as internally within D and E (G is easier), matters.

The same applies to CPF in health—how much are you allocating in your overall diet? People often say they are eating protein, but what percentage does it form in the grand scheme of your diet? The percentage you allocate is going to define your level of success, and that can only come from a basic understanding of macronutrient allocation.

Here's an interesting snippet from a Harvard Health article.[11]

In the 1960s, studies funded by the Sugar Research Foundation found that cholesterol and fat were the main contributors to weight gain, and were responsible for coronary heart disease. With fat removed from most foods, it had to be substituted with carbs (i.e., sugar) to make up for taste and appeal. You will remember that fat has more calories per gram (9) than carbs (4).

So, overall, the calorie count would have gone down, right? Wrong! The quantities you eat also matter here.

Moreover, many carbohydrates come with something called a high glycaemic index. This means that excess consumption of carbohydrates leads to an unnecessary increase in blood sugar levels, increasing your insulin levels to bring down that rise in blood sugar. Over time, if done frequently, this can result in insulin resistance, which can eventually lead to type-2 diabetes due to the body not having enough insulin to bring down high blood sugar. More on this will be covered in the next chapter—how excesses can lead to issues with our health and wealth.

The point is that fat cannot be demonized purely because of its high calorie count. It serves a purpose, and the quantity one consumes also matters.

To sum it up, we gravitate towards a balanced allocation. Nothing extreme, and we will do just fine.

Focus on the Process

'Create structure so you can have freedom. Map your direction, so you can swerve in the lane,' wrote Hollywood actor Matthew McConaughey in his book *Greenlights*.[12]

We hope this chapter has given you that basic structure, the direction. Remember to focus on only the factors in your control when you are swerving in the lane. You will get a sense that this book is going to make no false promises on how to get rich or fit, but it will give you a basic sense of direction.

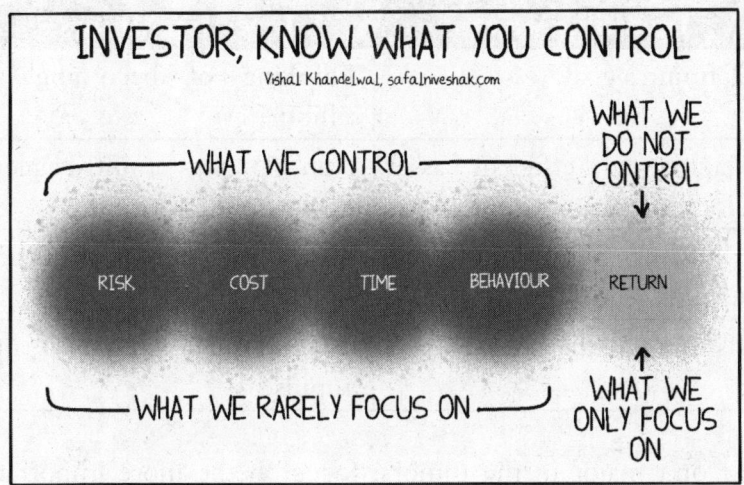

Source: Safal Niveshak[13]

The health aspect of this is simple—you control your overall calories and allocation within CPF. You also control other factors such as sleep and exercise. The end result of your weight, blood markers or clothing size is just a byproduct of the plan. These are all outcomes of focussing on a plan.

Fitness and Nutrition Majors	Fitness and Nutrition Minors
Calorie maintenance by focussing on quality	Trying to pick superfoods
Customizing the right macros	Worrying about fats/carbs
Sleep, nutrition, exercise	Supplements
Consistency	Hacks

Investing Majors	Investing Minors
Defining a goal	Thinking of becoming a billionaire
Making an efficient asset allocation plan	Hunting for multi-bagger stocks
Following a simple boring plan for years	Buying the hottest new fund or stock
Planning luxury purchases	Buying out of FOMO or impulse

Don't major in the minors; focus on the more important factors moving the needle and you will be on a positive path. Don't jump over dollars to pick up pennies. We end this chapter with a quote from investment and lifestyle guru Tim Ferriss that covers the first principles. 'Make a decision that can save you from a thousand decisions.'[14]

Key Principles Learned from This Chapter

- Focus on pinning down the first principles of an investing or nutrition plan.
- Customize each plan by changing the allocation as per your goals.
- Don't replicate someone else's plan because they saw success. You have to define your 'why' with your plan.

2

Invisible to the Naked Eye

Health and wealth are invisible to the naked eye. Would you consider these traits to be the epitome of health—a lean six pack, a tiny waist, a ripped physique.

If you answered 'yes' to all three, think again. Pictures never tell the full story.

Ankush's Story

In August 2021, I was in the best shape of my life. My gym performance was at its peak, my abs were chiselled, I broke personal lifting records every week and my food intake was optimal. My physical health seemed sorted. Or so I thought.

I got a wake-up call when I lost a cousin in his early thirties to a sudden heart attack.

He had worked hard, was one of the brightest people I knew and was building a great career in the tech world, but he didn't actively exercise or monitor his diet. He looked just fine—there had been no visible signs of something going wrong.

Now, my own father had had bypass surgery in the past, but to me, that hadn't been as relatable as the loss of my cousin. People need relatable stories to be jolted into making a change.

The loss of my cousin made me wonder if my body was truly doing alright on the inside, as I had read about a lot of individuals my age suffering on the health front despite looking enviable.

Could there be anything I could do to reduce the risk of a sudden heart attack or stroke? After all, it's not an uncommon occurrence even among super-fit groups like athletes and actors. And even if there were things that could be done, how would a layman like me even get to know?

I decided to do some research on my own, and considering my family history of diabetes and heart disease, consulted a doctor as well. Everyone has heard that genetic diseases are passed on to the kin, so I had to be doubly sure.

The first step, in August 2021, was to get a comprehensive blood test, which included a complete cholesterol test, also known as lipid profile.

The results were revealing. Despite being in my best physical shape, with just 11 per cent body fat (indicative of athlete-level fitness), my total cholesterol levels were high. It meant that my physical appearance was hiding a crucial fact about my heart health. I was not metabolically the healthiest person, despite having well-defined abs and a sculpted physique. I had high cholesterol, which you wouldn't have guessed from looking at me.

With help from the doctor, I got to work on my internal health and correcting the blood markers. After several ups and downs over eleven months, I managed to get it right.

Cholesterol gets a bad rep, but it isn't as evil as we may believe. It's a waxy substance that our body needs to build cells, produce hormones and make vitamins—it's essential to life, but in the right quantity. The cholesterol in our blood comes from two sources, the liver and the food we eat.

For processing foods that are high in saturated and trans fats, our liver needs to produce more cholesterol than the body requires. In some people, this excess cholesterol can veer toward unhealthy levels.

Most cholesterol is found in our cells, supporting essential biological functions, and about 7 per cent floats in our blood. Of this 7 per cent, one-third is supposed to be 'good' cholesterol, and two thirds is supposed to be 'bad' cholesterol. Well, it's not really the cholesterol that is good or bad, but its outer layer that helps in its transportation that the label should be applied to.

That there are two types of cholesterol is why getting a complete lipid profile is important—an imbalance between the two types is risky for your heart, and monitoring your stats could help prevent a sudden mishap.

What's also crucial is to remember that there is no fixed formula that can predict why exactly someone's heart would fail.

In his bestselling book *The Body*, Bill Bryson wrote, 'All forms of heart failure can be cruelly sneaky. For about a quarter of victims, the first (and, more unfortunately, last) time they know they have a heart problem is when they suffer a fatal heart attack. No less appallingly, more than half of all first heart attacks (fatal or otherwise) occur in people who are fit and healthy and have no known obvious risks. They don't smoke or drink excessively, are not seriously overweight, and do not have chronically high blood pressure or even bad cholesterol readings, but they get a heart attack anyway. Living a virtuous life doesn't guarantee you will escape heart problems; it just improves your chances.'[1]

I agree with Bryson, and I'd learnt my lesson only after losing someone. Such is the psychology of health.

While nothing can guarantee the absence of heart failure, keeping my total cholesterol levels under 200 mg/dl would help minimize the risk.

With the guidance of my doctor, I got my blood tests done and got an idea of what blood markers are crucial for me to track. Again, for readers who are not medical practitioners, the usual disclaimer applies—follow your own process but consult a doctor; take their view if you are researching on your own.

Reading a blood test report can be confusing. When I started, I only knew that if a certain reading was in bold, it meant it wasn't in the correct range. But I did not know what it meant. I realized it's not that complicated—there are five key things you need to know to understand your test results.

How's Cholesterol Measured?

Cholesterol is measured in milligrams per decilitre (mg/dl). When you check your cholesterol, the lipid profile test contains the levels of cholesterol and triglycerides in your body.

Good Cholesterol Versus Bad Cholesterol

Our body has two types of cholesterol: low-density lipoprotein cholesterol (LDLC) and high-density lipoprotein cholesterol (HDLC). The first, often referred to as 'bad cholesterol', makes up most of your total cholesterol levels; its desired level is below 120 mg/dl. Meanwhile, HDLC, often called 'good cholesterol', should be between 40 and 60 mg/dl.

However, the simplistic classification of HDLC and LDLC as 'good' and 'bad' respectively isn't accurate. Both types of cholesterol are the same; what's different is the protein composition of the outer layer and the roles these proteins play in our bodies—HDL carries cholesterol from the body to the liver for disposal, while LDL helps cells absorb cholesterol to perform important microbiological functions.[2]

The problem with LDL—and why it's called 'bad'—is that it can form a thick, hard deposit on the insides of our arteries. This narrows the arteries over time, making them less flexible. If a blood clot forms and blocks one of these narrowed arteries, it can result in a stroke or heart attack.

Triglycerides

This is fat stored as unused calories, and provides your body with energy. If you regularly eat more calories than your body requires your body starts storing a lot of unused calories, and your triglyceride levels could keep increasing. High triglycerides are a 'silent' killer, and there is a four-fold increase in the chances of a heart attack due to this.[3]

Triglyceride levels above 150 mg/dl are considered high, and what's worse, it's invisible to the naked eye till you get that blood test.

Total Cholesterol

This is the total amount of cholesterol in your blood based on your HDL, LDL and triglyceride numbers. In adults, high cholesterol means having total cholesterol above 200 mg/dL.

Ratios Help Predict the Risk of Heart Disease

There are two significant ratios to track in the blood report—LDLC to HDLC, and triglycerides to HDLC. The lower the ratios, the better it is. The ideal range for LDLC:HDLC is between 3.5:1 to 1:1, while the triglyceride:HDLC ratio should remain below 2:1.

My doctor asked me to change my lifestyle after looking at my initial test results. For one, he asked me to introduce more good-quality carbs into my diet to feel more nourished and follow a balanced approach. I'd been on a low-carb diet up to this point. Going low on carbs means the diet is dominated by proteins and fats, which are more satiating than carbs. This, in turn, means we tend not to binge on more calories, which helps in maintaining a low body fat percentage, which is needed for those abs to visibly show.

Second, the doctor also asked me to monitor my alcohol intake. I used to go out drinking with my friends every other weekend, and drink three to four large pegs. Most young corporate professionals carry this habit into older ages too. The doctor suggested this too could have led to elevated LDL levels.

Most professionals in their twenties and early thirties should heed this as a warning—we all compromise our health for social events, but sooner or later this habit comes back to bite us.

First Phase: August 2021 to March 2022

Things did not get better immediately, or even for many months. My March 2022 report showed a further rise in LDLC levels. The reason? Alcohol. Yes, I was working on improving my cholesterol levels, but I fell for the fear of missing out (FOMO) socially, and could not resist.

This, FOMO, is one of the key problems that most corporate professionals face early on in their careers.

Sleep was another possible factor. My bed timings were off point, which disrupted the total number of hours I got on many days. Some days I slept much more than needed.

Both of these factors led to poor body recovery, leading to poorer quality workouts. The results showed up in a less-than-optimal second blood test in March 2022.

Second Phase: March 2022 to August 2022

Finally, by August 2022, my blood report improved, showing a lower LDLC level, lower total cholesterol and improved HDL/

LDL parameters. It took a whole year of working on things, but the situation has never been better, and I'm not even missing out on the joys of social gatherings. Here is what worked for me.

Controlled Drinking

Between March and August 2022, I went cold turkey for drinks on the alternate weekends I used to go out. I have worked on this habit now and learnt to control social FOMO.

Found a Middle Ground for My Diet

As mentioned before, I'd been following a low-carb, high-protein diet with a sixteen-hour fasting period (based on convincing research and case studies available on the internet). While this improved my triglyceride/HDL ratio, it also led to an increase in my LDL. But while some research said that this in itself is not necessarily a bad thing, others said reducing LDL is critical.

So, what could I do? My target was to bring my LDL below 100 mg/dL while ensuring that my triglyceride/HDL and LDL/HDL ratios remained healthy. So, as per my doctor's advice, I took the middle ground. I introduced gradual changes and started taking in more calories (within a limit, of course—just more than what I was eating earlier) to accommodate more carbs in my diet while keeping my protein intake consistent. I specifically increased my complex carb intake—whole grains, for example.

The August 2022 blood report suggested this possibly worked. It's all about trial and error.

Changed My Cooking Oil

I paid attention to the quantity of oil being used but the quality of the oil matters equally. I used to cook my food in refined rice bran or sunflower oil. This is not a good idea. I switched to cooking all my foods in cold-pressed coconut oil or ghee, and occasionally in cold-pressed groundnut oil.

Coconut oil reportedly nudges up HDLC levels.[4]

Remember, the benefits of a protein-rich and home-cooked meal could get negated by choosing the wrong type of oil to cook it in. Include healthy fats and proteins as a part of your meals as they help to keep cholesterol in check.

Started to Focus on My Sleep

Lack of sleep is known to cause an increase in cholesterol levels.[5] In addition, a study showed that individuals who get less than six hours of sleep see a rise in their LDLC and triglyceride levels.

Heart diseases are sneaky—they don't announce, they just arrive. I learned this the hard way, unfortunately through the experience of my cousin. How could I do justice to his memory? Make this change in my own life, and spread awareness to others.

It's important to keep a tab on your blood markers (even if you look healthy), consult a doctor when in doubt, and see what works to keep you healthy.

Mihir's Story

I was thirty, under the impression that I was in the prime of my health. After all, I went to the gym, ate 'healthy', my waist size wasn't out of the ordinary, and I looked 'fit'. There was no reason for me to even get a check-up. Or so I thought.

It all began with my wife complaining about how irritable I was—I would snap at anything and anyone, and get worked up very easily. It took thirty seconds to hook me up to the blood pressure monitor at home, and it read 150/100 mmHg—an extremely dangerous level at my age. I shrugged it off, saying, 'This isn't baseline; this is just an elevated reading since I am worked up.'

Turns out I was wrong. The next morning, it was at the same level, and SOS calls were made to doctors in my family, who went into overdrive, prescribing a few hundred tests.

Here's what was brewing inside me, beneath the 'healthy' surface.

- Hypertension
- Onset of fatty liver (even though I very rarely indulge in a drink)
- High cholesterol

My cardiologist immediately put me on statins and blood pressure medications, had my eyes checked (high blood pressure can apparently affect optic nerves too), and banned everything that I liked to eat—eggs, shellfish, cheese, oil, butter, peanuts; heck, even rice! He said, 'Once you start BP meds, they continue for life. Make sure you don't miss a dose.'

I went about changing my diet anecdotally. For example, I cut out sugar at first, because everyone said sugar is bad. I lost about 2 kg in a month just by cutting out sugar. Slowly, I took it to the next level by cutting out junk like farsan (Indian salty snacks) and biscuits. However, that only helped me reduce another kilo. There was no impact on my BP and cholesterol yet, and I just ended up feeling deprived of eating things I liked. After all, cabbage isn't half as interesting as black pepper crab or butter chicken.

Coincidentally, around the same time, my cousin Dr Amit Prabhu happened to visit us. His first question was, 'Can you arrange paneer, peanuts and eggs for me while I am there?'

I was surprised by the odd request, but of course, I arranged it all for him. When he arrived, he looked like a boy—not just young, but fit. Underneath his size 'M' T-shirt, he had washboard abs—the kind we had seen on screen since we were kids. It took only a two-hour session with him for me to understand what worked for him. We built a lifestyle plan—not a diet plan—for me. It has just two key elements: the quantum of calories I eat, and the composition of the source of those calories (carbs, protein and fats). This involved eating everything I liked—eggs, chicken, ghee, peanuts and even an occasional cupcake.

I started exercising at home. My wife joined in on both the eating plan and the exercise. We trained our cook to make calorie-counted and calorie-composed meals. It took us two months to be able to do 100 push-ups easily.

Eight months in, and I was down 18 kg, while my wife was down 10 kg. Boom! We discovered the secret—calorie counting, exercise, adequate sleep and adequate water intake. This seems to be an oversimplification, but it is a simple concept, the implementation of which is not easy.

Case in point, a doctor cousin of mine was getting married, and his mother gave me a customary box of *peda* after the rituals concluded. I couldn't resist the snide remark, 'Couldn't you have found cocaine instead?' Luckily, I survived that one because my aunt broke into a laugh and admired me for my discipline rather than take offence.

Prevention Is Better Than Cure

The modern world defines a healthy person according to their waist size, the protrusion of their belly, the bulge of their biceps or how many packs of abs are visible. However, this definition is far from true. As you can see from our stories, waist size doesn't really define the worth of health.

Dr Peter Attia is an author and physician who focusses on prevention before cure. In his book *Outlive* he mentions that

if an individual meets three or more of the conditions listed below, they are considered metabolically unhealthy:[6]
1. High blood pressure (over 130/85 mmHg)
2. High triglycerides (over 150 mg/dl)
3. Lower HDL cholesterol (under 40 mg/dl in men, or under 50 mg/dl in women)
4. Central adiposity (waist circumference over 40 inches in men, or over 35 inches in women)
5. Elevated fasting glucose (over 110 mg/dl)
6. High LDL cholesterol (over 100 mg/dl)

Some doctors would have a different view on each blood marker's ideal range, but these are the general ones we can track to begin with, and then consult our doctors if we spot something wrong.

Notice in the list above that waist circumference is only one of the criteria—the problem lies beyond just how thin or fat a person is. In fact, a study done with 3,81,000 participants found that approximately one-third of people who are obese by the standards of the Body Mass Index (BMI) are actually metabolically healthy, using the same parameters to define metabolic syndrome. So, people of our grandparents' generation who did not meet the BMI criteria could possibly have been metabolically healthy.[7]

The process we followed is to first make our new lifestyle a habit that can sustain for a lifetime, before popping pills to cure the problem. The former is harder, but the harder it is to do, the better the outcome is going to be.

Also, in the book *Outlive*, Attia emphasizes the need for prevention by giving the Biblical example of Noah's ark.[8]

'When did Noah build the ark? Long before it began to rain. Medicine 2.0, which is a pure treatment approach, tries to figure out how to get dry after it starts raining. Medicine 3.0, which is a prevention-before-treatment approach, studies meteorology and tries to determine whether we need to build a better roof or a boat.'

The world manufactures new definitions of what it means to be healthy every other day, and adds to the existing anxiety. But the human body pretty much remains the same, and following set principles is really the simpler way to better health.

As long as we are clear about what true health really is.

The Case of Wealth

Have a look at the person posing for the picture in front of their supercar. You would assume they are the epitome of wealth, right?

We hope you have some idea where this is headed.

When we see someone driving a nice car, we rarely think, 'Wow, the guy driving that car is cool.' Instead, we think, 'Wow, if I had that car, people would think I'm cool.'

Subconscious or not, this is how people think.

As Morgan Housel wrote in *The Psychology of Money*, 'The paradox of wealth is that people tend to want it to signal to others that they should be liked and admired. But in reality, those other people bypass admiring you, not because they don't think wealth is admirable, but because they use your wealth solely as a benchmark for their own desire to be liked and admired.'[9]

In the interest of confidentiality, I (Ankush) would like to highlight a real-life instance illustrating this without naming the person or disclosing my relationship with them. This individual possesses a collection of cars, a large house and a well-established family. At first glance, it would be easy to assume that this person is thriving—I might even aspire to have a life like theirs one day.

Now as I peel the layers like an onion, I find the dark spots.

This person has been taking loans to fund their lavish lifestyle. They go ahead and buy a car, and plan to take a home loan to move to a bigger, swankier apartment. This person is only focussed on today's lifestyle and not too worried about how that loan will be serviced. They are too deeply invested in flaunting their lifestyle, and all of us from the outside world envy it.

After many years, this person is scrambling to borrow money from friends and family to pay off all those loans, but one thing continues—the extravagant lifestyle—because it is the image they wish to maintain.

Poor habits, when it comes to health and wealth, manifest negatively in our lives at a later stage, when it is too late to reverse them.

Let us use another analogy here to explain the concept of not judging a book by its cover with that of a green, unripe mango. When we buy a green mango that is unripe, even if we drop it a few times, the damage will not be visible because the mango blackens from the inside, not the outside. Compare this mango to another green mango that has not been dropped, and you will see that both mangoes look identical. Now, when both mangoes ripen and turn orange, once we cut them open to eat, we will see that the first mango, which was dropped multiple times, has blackened completely and must be thrown away, while the second mango, which was not dropped, is juicy, orange and ready to eat.

Diderot's Scarlet Robe and Other Stories

It is in the psychological nature of human beings to purchase items with the intention of impressing others, termed the Diderot effect. According to this phenomenon, acquiring a new possession frequently triggers a cycle of consumption, compelling individuals to accumulate more new things, which leads to a cycle of never being happy with what we have and always wanting more.

James Clear, in his book *Atomic Habits*, has highlighted the Diderot effect through the story of the man who originally described it, and whom it is named after—eighteenth century French philosopher Denis Diderot.[11]

Diderot endured financial hardship throughout much of his life, until a pivotal moment in 1765. Confronted with the daunting expenses of his daughter's upcoming wedding, Diderot, despite his renown as a distinguished writer and the visionary behind the *Encyclopédie*, found himself unable to meet the financial demands. It was during this trying time that Catherine the Great, Empress of Russia, happened to read the *Encyclopédie*, which she thoroughly enjoyed. She learned of Diderot's predicament and empathized with him.

Sharing his passion for literature, she made a generous proposition: to purchase Diderot's personal library for 15,000 francs (which, adjusted for inflation today, would amount to approximately 150,000 francs), a gesture that profoundly altered the course of his life.[12]

With this windfall, Diderot was not only able to cover the expenses for his daughter's wedding, he even acquired a scarlet robe for himself. This robe, standing out amid his modest possessions, prompted him to reconsider his belongings. Feeling the urge for a transformation, he began to upgrade his possessions one by one—purchasing a rug from Damascus, acquiring expensive sculptures, replacing his humble kitchen table with an extravagant one and his modest straw chair with a luxurious leather one. Diderot spared no expense. Soon, he had no money left, and discovered that his newfound wealth had only served to fuel an insatiable desire for more, leaving him perpetually discontented.

Take these two stories from *The Psychology of Money* by Morgan Housel to show how true wealth is invisible to the naked eye.[13]

Grace Groner was orphaned at age twelve. She never married, never had kids, never drove a car. She lived most of her life alone in a one-bedroom house and worked her whole career as a secretary. She was, by all accounts, a lovely lady. But she lived a humble and quiet life. That made the $7 million she left to charity after her death in 2010, at age 100, all the more confusing. People who knew her asked, 'Where did Grace get all that money?'

But there was no secret. There was no inheritance. Grace took humble savings from a meagre salary and enjoyed eighty years of hands-off compounding in the stock market. That was it. There was no show of money, just the money being put to work.

Richard Fuscone, former vice-chairman of a very large bank's Latin America division, declared personal bankruptcy, fighting off foreclosure on two homes, one of which was nearly 20,000 square feet and had a $66,000 monthly mortgage.[14] Fuscone was the opposite of Grace Groner—educated at Harvard and the University of Chicago, he became so successful in the investment industry that he retired in his forties to 'pursue personal and charitable interests'. But heavy borrowing and illiquid investments did him in. The same year Grace Groner left a veritable fortune to charity, Fuscone stood before a bankruptcy judge and declared: 'I have been devastated by the financial crisis. The only source of liquidity is whatever my wife is able to sell in terms of personal furnishings.'

The purpose of these stories is not to say we should be like Groner and that Fuscone is a villain, but to show that when it comes to wealth, it is impossible to judge a book by its cover.

I (Ankush) have spent years working in the investment management industry, and have interacted with a large set of ultra-high-net-worth individuals who carry themselves in such a way that you wouldn't believe their net worth. Probably a large part of their success is shaped by some form of frugality, a strong level of self-satisfaction, and not having the urge to live their own lives for the attention of others. It's a fool's errand to judge someone without knowing the contours of what lies within.

We tend to admire the fastest-growing companies, the wealthiest individuals and the most athletic of persons, and then, unthinkingly, make these the measuring rods for success. There is nothing wrong in doing so, but the key tenet to remember that the processes they used to achieve their goals could be entirely different from ours.

Don't forget that these athletes, investors and companies could be resorting to unfair ways of achieving their goals too, and their accomplishments could paint a false picture of what success looks like.

To the world, external appearances may paint a rosy picture, but what is happening behind the scenes is completely out of our vision—there could be a disaster in the making, and the collapse could be inevitable, swift and painful.

Jim Collins, in his book *How the Mighty Fall*, writes, 'I've come to see institutions decline like a staged disease: harder to detect but easier to cure in the earlier stages, easier to detect but harder to cure in the late stages. An institution can look strong on the outside but already be sick on the inside, dangerously on the cusp of a precipitous fall.'[15]

Wealth is subjective to each person, but due to the power of envy, we tend to make the mistake of painting everyone with the same brush. Many products and services are designed in such a way that they want to make us envious of the person 'above' us.

Invisible to the Naked Eye

There are a million ways to get healthy and wealthy, and plenty of books on how to do so. But there's only one way to stay both wealthy and healthy—understanding our own limitations, working on them, and not being envious of others' outward appearances.

The late Charlie Munger, legendary teacher and investor, who lived till the age of ninety-nine and was Warren Buffet's partner, stood by this quote fiercely over multiple decades, 'It's not greed that drives the world, but envy.'[16]

Or, for the *Star Wars* buffs out there, it's like Master Yoda points out, 'Attachment leads to jealousy. The shadow of greed, that is.'

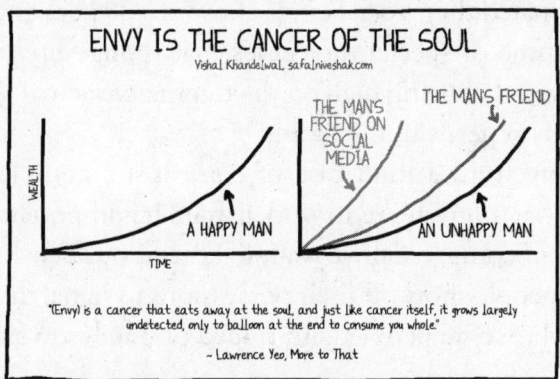

Source: Vishal Khandelwal, Safalniveshak.com[17]

While we think envy is a 'human' emotion, but this is far from the truth. Animals also suffer from envy.

Jason Zweig, in his book *Your Money and Your Brain*, dug deep into this research. Animals often show higher levels of stress when they are in a 'lower' status in their circle.[18] When a mouse is intimidated by a more powerful member of the group, its brain produces extra amounts of protein that enhance memory, encouraging future 'social defeat'. Rats that are low in their group's pecking order tend to lose their appetite, become lethargic and sleep fitfully, and their adrenal glands become enlarged. Fish, when their territory is dominated by another member of the same school, shut down production of a protein that enhances fertility. The less 'real estate they own', the less likely they are to reproduce.

Neurobiologist Michael Platt used fruit juice as currency to test the envy hypothesis on monkeys, and found that they tended to spend more of their 'currency' to look at pictures of monkeys higher in the pecking order; and conserved the currency and avoided looking at those below them on the social ladder. After three months, it was observed that the monkeys who dominated their social circle showed a 20 per cent increase in the volume of special molecules that sponge up dopamine. This showed that being high on the totem pole actually beefs up the rewards systems in the brain.[19]

Suffering from a mild case of comparison complex can be beneficial—it motivates us to work harder. It is important to know what kind of comparison we want to keep as our benchmark.

Just as people show off their possessions to signal their wealth to the public, so do people with ripped physiques to signal their health.

Someone driving a car worth one crore rupees might be wealthy, but the only actual data point we have about their wealth is that they have a crore rupees less than before. It's as Morgan Housel puts it, 'It is easy to find rich role models; it is harder to find wealthy ones because by definition their success is more hidden.'[20]

The Psychology of Social Media

It is important to address the psychology of social media in this chapter, because a number of people today derive their definitions of health and wealth from it.

Instagram is perhaps the headquarters of human narcissism, and the writer George Mack has a beautiful take on it, which he calls 'Instagram's Razor'. 'When you see a photo of an influencer looking attractive on Instagram—assume there are ninety-nine worse variations of that photo you haven't seen. They just picked the best one.'[21]

Inspired by this, I (Ankush) have a similar take on Twitter (now X). 'When you see a person posting pictures of their profits on a stock or fund, assume there are ninety-nine other photos where the person has made a big loss. They just picked the best one.'

We must point out here that what is relevant even today is a quote by the ancient Greek philosopher Epictetus, 'Self-sufficiency is the greatest of all wealth. Wealth consists not in having great possessions, but in having few wants.'[22]

Key Principles Learned from This Chapter

- Health and wealth are invisible to the naked eye—what we see is far from reality.
- Health and fitness are not the same, but both depend on each other. Wealth and money are not the same, but both depend on each other. The level of dependency will vary from person to person.
- We tend to take measures to protect our money, because we know the cost. Same with our fitness, which can be tangibly measured. But 'health' and 'wealth' are much broader concepts, and may not be as well defined as we think they are.

3

Less Is More

The secret of happiness, you see, is not found in seeking more, but in developing the capacity to enjoy with less.

Socrates[1]

In the opening chapter, we covered what constitutes effective allocations for nutrition and investing.

By now, the following simple formulae should be familiar to you.

1. BMR < 4P+4C+9F < TEE
2. 4P:4C:9F = x:y:z

And

1. Income – Investing = Spending
2. D:E:G = x:y:z

In this chapter, using these formulae to further our understanding of health and wealth, we delve into why 'avoiding' things is a more effective strategy than 'choosing', and how you can use planned allocation techniques to avoid blunders in your journey.

Mathematically, this couldn't get simpler. Consume fewer calories than you burn. And maximize your income and investing to minimize your spending.

But human psychology doesn't make things easy for us. This brings us to two ways to adhere to our base formulae:

1. Either eat less or burn more.
2. Either spend less or earn more.

Burning more and earning more is more difficult than eating less and spending less.

In his book *The Body*, Bill Bryson writes, 'One study in America found that people overestimated the number of calories they burned in a workout by a factor of four. They also then consumed, on average, about twice as many calories as they had just burned off. The fact is, you can quickly undo a lot of exercise by eating a lot of food, and most of us do.'[2,3] If we eat calories and do not use them productively, we are going to put on fat and depreciate the value of our bodies over time. On the income front, the more we earn and the less we productively use it, the more the value of our money depreciates.

Let's explain with the example of calories in and calories out.

After dedicating an hour to the treadmill, you burn approximately 400 calories, which gives you a sense of accomplishment.

The sweat, the soreness in your legs, the rush of endorphins—all signal a successful workout.

You feel you have now earned your next treat. Your food delivery app sends you a notification on the best options; the hunger from hitting the treadmill makes you think irrationally.

You tell yourself you'll only indulge a little, maybe just a bite.

Yet, as the sugar rushes to your brain, you find yourself devouring the entire treat, rationalizing it with, 'After an hour of running, I deserve this much, at least.'

You end up consuming 800 calories in just ten minutes, a mere fraction of the hour you spent burning 400 of them. That leaves you with a surplus of 400 calories.

In hindsight, skipping the treadmill itself would have been the better choice. A simple walk would have sufficed, as you would have probably not assumed that you burnt so much.

In no way are we disincentivizing a workout, but sometimes we tend to focus on the wrong things when trying to achieve our goals.

It is easier to skip a decadent, high-calorie treat than to eat it and then attempt to burn it off. The time as well as the effort needed to burn excess calories isn't worth it.

Here's a chart of some of people's favourite foods and how long it takes to burn them off. This gives us a broad-level understanding by matching calories with activity, and illustrates why simply eating less would be a much better strategy.[4]

Food	Quantity	Calories	Time needed to burn (running at 8 km/h)
Sugar drink	100 ml	138	13 minutes
Chocolate bar	50 g	276	26 minutes
Loaded sandwich	2 pieces	500	50 minutes
Large pizza	4 pieces	650	1 hour and 16 minutes

(Disclaimer: This is just for illustrative purposes, to help understand how calories work. Before we enrage any nutritionists reading this, efficiency can vary based on one's metabolism. Assuming the weight of the person and the BMR are kept static, calories burnt can go up or down based on weight, metabolism and type of activity, be it resistance training or endurance training. This is more of a directional chart on the importance of avoiding junk, rather than directions on how to burn it off.)

The foods in the chart will barely even satiate you due to the lack of fibre in processed foods and you will end up looking to 'burn off' those calories out of guilt. This can turn into a vicious cycle.

Have a look at the following whole and natural foods and their calorie counts.

Food	Quantity	Calories
Boneless chicken	200 g	228
Basa fish	300 g	177
Dahi	300 g	180
Paneer	200 g	200

Source: MyFitnessPal app

The good news is that if you make a plan for your calorie intake, as we did, then you can indulge in some high-calorie junk foods. But if you don't have a plan or direction in place, then make sure to carry your running shoes with you at all times.

This is how the basics of calories in and calories out work. We'll delve further into our understanding of the topic of metabolism in a subsequent chapter.

Now, let's see how a similar system of first principles thinking can help us take account of spending habits.

Time Taken to Earn vs Time Taken to Spend

As the month comes to a close, that much-awaited notification lights up the phone. 'xxx amount has been credited to your bank account.'

We have worked hard for this monetary reward.

We now have ample liquidity to splurge.

This liquidity makes us overlook the value of what's being purchased. Perhaps it's a depreciating gadget, a product that sways us by enticing discounts rather than necessity, or an impulse buy that adds to an inflated credit card bill.

We are not at all advocating any form of minimalism—we use expensive phones, smartwatches and top-of-the-line laptops.

But these purchases are planned, sometimes over years, in a manner that doesn't disrupt the larger investment plan.

The plan is made in such a way that, let's say, our salary increases by 10 per cent over the year. The systematic investment plan (SIP) amount is also automatically adjusted upwards by 10 per cent to ensure there is a balance between income and expenditure.

So, before you think of us as soulless creatures who don't enjoy the good things that life has to offer, let us tell you that we are middle-class individuals who have woken up to the reality that prudent spending is one of the underrated tools in the journey of wealth creation. This is probably why you picked up this book as well, isn't it?

Increase TEE before allowing yourself the luxury of consuming more avoidable calories; similarly, increase your income before allowing yourself the luxury of increased, but avoidable, expenditure.

Neuroscientist Tali Sharot, in her book *The Optimism Bias*, explains how 'people hugely underestimate their chances of getting divorced, losing their job or being diagnosed with cancer; expect their children to be extraordinarily gifted; envision themselves achieving more than their peers; and overestimate their likely life span (sometimes by twenty years or more). Sharot calls this the Optimism Bias, which leads to irrational behavior.'[5]

Less Is More

While it's great to be optimistic, it also clouds our judgement about our fitness and investing journeys. We often overestimate the calories burnt, granting ourselves excessive credit for minimal exercise duration, and underestimate the calories consumed in our foods. Or, we overestimate returns we can make from a stock, getting stuck in the narrative that 'every popular investor is buying this stock', or 'the new CEO is a rockstar', or 'I use their products myself so it's a great company.' Eventually, we end up losing money. We've all been there, haven't we?

We also tend to underestimate investment risk, by wondering what's the worst that can happen.

Sometimes, optimism leads us to irrational decisions that make us stray from our path. Learning to be a realist first and having a plan in place, combined with optimism, is the way to go.

The whole world is looking to do something out of the box to achieve results, when in reality, not doing certain things is a much easier process to avoid ruin.

Here's what you shouldn't be doing:

Nutrition	Investing
Eating calorie-dense foods	Investing outside of your allocation
Not making a weekly plan	Acting on stock tips
Taking frequent 'cheat days'	Doing something because your 'smart' friend or colleague told you.

Again, this sounds surprisingly easy, but ironically, most people fail at maintaining this discipline because they do not have their basic first principles dialled in.

These are extremely simple ground rules, which can help take the first step towards success. Now let us look at all the steps listed in the aforementioned table one by one.

Nutrition To-Not-Dos

Eating Calorie-Dense Foods

Let's take the example of a potato chip packet, which has around 800–1,000 calories. This is equivalent to eight-ten bananas and yet the potato chips will not be able to satiate you as much as the bananas, which have fibre to keep you satiated for longer and well-nourished.

Here we are comparing a carbohydrate option with a carbohydrate option.

Processed food are stripped off their fibre to make you keep snacking more.

Like most ultra-processed foods, potato chips are carefully crafted with the 'holy trinity' of salt, sugar and fat to hack the reward circuitry of our brains and induce artificial cravings.

These foods keep the excitement of taste going, so people get easily addicted and overshoot their calories.[6]

Not Making a Weekly Plan

If we don't plan out our calorie intake in advance, we'll have a tough time managing each meal, and will eventually give up the process. Planning ensures that the stress of thinking 'what to eat for this meal' is taken out.

In my (Ankush's) case, for example, the weekly plan of 2,100 calories per day allows me to overshoot calories on a single day without feeling any guilt—I can adjust the plan accordingly.

Taking Frequent 'Cheat Days'

Not making that weekly plan eventually leads to multiple cheat days, which disrupts our entire nutrition plan. If the plan is for a weekly average of 2,000 calories a day and you eat 4,000 calories each on two of those days, that means you have five days remaining and only 6,000 calories left in your budget.

Investing To-Not-Dos

Investing Outside of Our Allocation

We make a plan to invest in a certain set of funds and stocks, but slowly we start adding a few more funds and stocks, just out of FOMO. This eventually hampers our overall plan, and we are left with an overflowing basket of investments.

Avoiding Derivatives

It takes a single bad day for derivatives to wipe out our entire capital.

'Smart' Friend or Colleague Said It

We think this person is smarter than us, so what they're doing must be right. But we have no idea about their investment framework, risk profile or motivation to buy the stock—it may be completely different to ours.

Most successful investing involves the process of elimination first, then selection. Eliminating junk companies at the start is winning 70 per cent of the battle; the remaining 30 per cent involves choosing the right companies. Nutrition involves the same principle—eliminate junk that comes out of a package and choose what quantities of whole and natural foods we need to include in our lifestyle.

Unfortunately, though, one always ends up asking 'where do I invest?' or 'what should I eat to lose weight or reduce risk of heart disease?', rather than asking 'what shouldn't I be doing?'. Given the world of information overload we live in, and the available excesses in all aspects of life, it is much easier to focus on what not to do. Once we remove the negatives, we are only left with what is good for us.

In my (Ankush's) profession, my fund manager typically filters out companies and sectors that the client should not invest into first, and comes up with a limited number of companies before deciding on all the companies to invest in by creating a strict investment philosophy.

Let's return to the legends of investing, Charlie Munger and Warren Buffet, for their advice on this matter. 'Tell me where I die and I will never go there,' says Munger.[7] Buffet adds, 'The difference between successful people and really successful people is that really successful people say no to almost everything.'[8]

In his book *What I Learned About Investing from Darwin*, Pulak Prasad, founder and fund manager of the exceptionally successful Nalanda Capital, highlights a very important lesson that his fund focusses on first: 'Avoid big losses.'[9]

Type 1 and Type 2 Errors

There are two types of errors in investing:

A Type 1 error occurs when one makes a poor investment decision, thinking it's a good one. It's also referred to as a false positive or an error of commission. This essentially means accepting the null hypothesis when, in reality, it's false.

A Type 2 error involves rejecting a potentially good investment because one believes it's a bad one. It's termed a false negative or an error of omission. This corresponds to rejecting the null hypothesis even though it's actually true.

It's important to note that reducing the risk of a Type 1 error often leads to an increase in the risk of a Type 2 error, and vice versa. Please pause and re-read this sentence while taking a few slow, deep breaths to fully grasp the information before moving forward.

Prasad gives examples of how to reduce these errors through Darwinian evolution.

On Type 1, the error of commission, he uses the analogy of a deer drinking from a watering hole. If it chooses to drink, it exposes itself to the risk of being attacked by a crocodile or a predator in hiding, like a tiger. The deer has learned through years of evolution and ancestral lineages that if it is overly cautious, hydration will become an issue, but if it becomes too careless, it's instant death. Unlike us, who are only risking our money, the deer is risking its life every single time at the watering hole. Over millions of years, it has learnt how to navigate this risk, lest it become extinct.

Now, in the process of minimizing Type 1 errors, the deer exposes itself to the risk of a Type 2 error—a deer might not be able to run fast enough to evade a tiger in the jungle if it is not adequately hydrated. This situation arises when the deer chooses to forgo visiting the watering hole due to its fear of the tiger.

The deer has to navigate between these two types of errors to ensure survival.

This simple analogy can be further applied specifically to filtering stocks.

Prasad illustrates why prioritizing rejection should come before selection by using data gathered from the pool of 4,000 listed companies in the United States in 2018.

A competent investor would assume that about 25 per cent of these opportunities qualify as 'good investments'.

Consequently, we can estimate that there are approximately 1,000 good investments, leaving the remaining 3,000 to be categorized as poor investments.

Prasad highlights a scenario where you encounter a star investor who claims she has a method to accurately identify these good investments; she claims she is accurate 80 per cent of the time. This implies that when encountering a bad investment, she will reject it correctly 80 per cent of the time, and when encountering a good investment, she will choose it accurately 80 per cent of the time.

However, while this looks logical, it's not mathematically true—the investor's correct prediction rate is actually 57 per cent, not 80 per cent.

Considering that there are 1,000 good investments, and given that this investor makes Type 2 errors 20 per cent of the time, she will correctly identify and select 800 companies from this list of good investments. Now, in the market, there exist 3,000 bad investments too. Due to Type 1 errors occurring 20 per cent of the time, she will incorrectly classify 600 companies from this list as 'good investments'.

Consequently, the total count of investments she considers 'good' becomes 1,400. But only 800 of these are actually 'good', so her probability of being right is just over half, or 57 per cent.

Now, let's analyse a situation where the investor reduces her Type 2 errors from 20 per cent to 10 per cent while maintaining her Type 1 error rate at 20 per cent.

Out of the 1,000 good investments, she correctly selects 900, and out of the 3,000 bad investments, she wrongly considers 600 as good.

So, her accuracy rises by only three percentage points to 60 per cent (900 out of 1,500 picks).

Suppose the investor is more adept at rejecting investments and decreases her Type 1 error rate from 20 per cent to 10 per cent. Consequently, she would only choose 300 bad investments from the pool of 3,000.

If her Type 2 error rate remains unchanged at 20 per cent, she accurately identifies 80 per cent of the good investments, resulting in the selection of 800 investments. Hence, out of the 1,100 investments she selects, 800 will actually be good, so her accuracy rises to a *whooping* 73 per cent.

In an extreme scenario where both Type 1 and Type 2 errors are reduced to 10 per cent, she would select 900 good investments and 300 bad ones, giving her a success rate of 75 per cent (900 out of 1,200).

Thus, we can see that the reduction of Type 1 errors leads to a more substantial improvement in the accuracy of identifying good investments.

By grasping the concept of Type 1 and Type 2 errors, we realize that the number of investments an investor perceives as good will likely be higher according to their expectations, compared to what aligns with reality.

'This underscores the argument that while investment literature and education emphasize selecting good investments, individuals would benefit more from understanding how to avoid poor investments,' writes Prasad.

I (Ankush) actually saw Prasad's theoretical explanation in action on a recent family holiday safari in the Masai Mara in Africa. Once lions hunt their prey and eat to their heart's content, they will wait for four or five days before they are ready for their next hunt. In this intervening period, they probably won't get tempted by prey around them, and will sit around lazing in the grass. A key lesson is that once we have a plan in place and are focussed on a goal, we can let things go and be happy to not do things that aren't part of the plan.

When it comes to nutrition, even foods deemed 'healthy' can be bad for us if consumed in excess. Anything in excess is unhealthy—just as we learnt in school about the results of overwatering plants.

Plants use carbon dioxide from the air and water from the soil to produce glucose through photosynthesis. This process involves combining CO_2 from the atmosphere and water (H_2O) in the presence of sunlight to create glucose and oxygen.

Excess of water and air would lead to excess glucose, resulting in the plant withering and die.

In the same way, humans get excess glucose through excess calories, which eventually can lead to chronic diseases.

Glucose is regulated by a hormone in our body called insulin. In her book *The Glucose Goddess Method*, Jesse Inchauspe explains the process of insulin by taking a cue from the video game Tetris.[10]

In Tetris, players arrange the pieces into rows to clear them before they block out the whole screen. It's eerily similar to what happens in our body—as too much glucose enters, our body does its best to stash it away.

The pancreas sends out insulin, whose sole purpose is to stash excess glucose in storage units throughout the body and keep it out of circulation.

Insulin stashes this glucose in several storage units, the first being the liver. This is the most convenient storage unit, because all the blood that comes from the gut carrying new glucose from digestion has to go through the liver.

The liver turns glucose into a new form called glycogen, equivalent to how plants turn glucose into starch. If excess glucose stayed in its original form, it would cause damage.

The liver can hold about 100 g of glucose in glycogen form (the amount of glucose in two large orders of fries). That's around half of the 200 g of glucose our body needs for energy per day.

The second storage unit are our muscles, and they are effective in this role because we have so many of them. The muscles of a typical adult weighing 68 kg can hold about 400 g of glucose as glycogen, or the amount of glucose in seven large orders of McDonald's fries.

So, if you've heard the saying that muscles protect us from putting on excess fat, this is the explanation—muscles are glucose storage units.

The fat our body creates has a few unfortunate destinies as per her:
1. It accumulates in the liver and could lead to the development of non-alcoholic fatty liver disease.
2. It fills up fat cells in our hips, thighs, face and between our organs, and we gain weight.
3. Lastly, it enters the bloodstream and contributes to the increased risk of heart disease through the formation of LDL cholesterol.

The above issues could occur due to a condition called insulin resistance, where so much insulin has been produced by the body that the pancreas loses the stamina to produce enough of it to temper the increases in blood glucose after a point.

Insulin becomes less sensitive to the intake of food, thereby allowing blood glucose to rise freely.

Once insulin has stored all the glucose it can in our liver and muscles, any excess glucose is turned into fat and fat reserves. That is where the problems begin. This solidifies the point that even excess of something good can be detrimental.

For an individual who is metabolically unhealthy, the calories they consume are often directed to areas where they are unnecessary or even get flushed out of their body.

The decision on where to put this energy in the body is taken by insulin.

Dr Peter Attia, in his book *Outlive*, describes four primary diseases that he compares to the Biblical 'Four Horsemen of the Apocalypse'.[11]

1. Diabetes and metabolic disease
2. Heart disease
3. Neurogenerative disorders
4. Cancer

Attia hypothesizes that these diseases are mostly caused by excesses, and any excess invites us to be chased down by these 'four horsemen'.

Diabetes and Metabolic Disease

Excess consumption of sugary and refined foods leads to insulin resistance, where cells fail to respond to insulin properly, causing elevated blood sugar levels. Over time, this can damage blood vessels and organs, leading to Type 2 diabetes.

Heart Disease

High intake of saturated fats and cholesterol-rich foods can raise levels of LDL (bad) cholesterol, leading to plaque build-up in arteries, narrowing them and reducing blood flow to the heart. This increases the risk of heart attacks and other cardiovascular problems.

Neurogenerative Disorders

Excessive consumption of processed foods high in trans fats and refined sugars can contribute to inflammation and oxidative stress in the brain, accelerating the progression of neurodegenerative diseases like Alzheimer's and Parkinson's.

Cancer

Consuming a diet high in processed meats, sugary beverages and foods with additives and preservatives can lead to chronic inflammation and DNA damage, increasing the risk of mutations and cancerous cell growth. Additionally, obesity resulting from excess calorie intake is a significant risk factor for various cancers.

While there could be multiple other factors responsible for these diseases, a large reason why they could be caused is due to excesses.

We have spoken about calories quite frequently in this chapter, but one aspect that you may miss out on while focussing on calories is maximizing nutrition per calorie.

How each calorie is broken down by our body is based on our metabolism—the process by which we take in nutrients and our body breaks them down for use.

This 'machine' runs smoothly when we give it the right raw materials.

This is why going into an extreme caloric deficit just for the sake of losing weight could hamper your metabolism.

Now, let's say you have started earning money and have received increment after increment. What do you do with that money? By now, you would have learned that setting aside a portion of that money for investing to grow your wealth would be a more sensible idea than letting it pile up in your bank account.

Excess savings will eventually become like excess fat, which depreciates the value of your body.

Calories are like salary; at the end of the day, being healthy is about how we put those calories to use, just as we put our salary to use to grow our wealth.

Much like the four horsemen of death when it comes to health, there are four horsemen of financial ruin in investing as well:

1. Intent
2. Leverage
3. Complicated products
4. Valuation

Intent

The beauty and drawback of buying stocks is that you own a piece of the company. The catch? You have no control over how it's run. It's like owning a car but being stuck in the backseat, relying on the driver to take you where you need to go. Will they drive safely? Will they actually reach the right destination?

When investing in stocks, you're always at the mercy of the promoter (owner). The promoters' intent must align with your goals. But intent isn't something you can take at face value. It's shown in the promoters' actions, not their words. Promoters' behaviour over time, particularly how they respect other shareholders' interests, reveals their true intent. Actions, not words about actions. And we are lucky here because actions (well, at least most of them) have consequences that can be observed in past financial statements.

So, how do you spot intent issues (financial red flags)? A key indicator is whether promoters treat themselves differently from minority shareholders. One can follow the money trail to deduce their intent. Some ways the money trail reveals intent are as follows:

1. *Capital expenditure:* Inflated costs or contracts for equipment or construction through related parties are signs of questionable intent.
2. *Revenue expenditure:* Paying themselves rent, funding personal lavish expenses, or engaging in unfair sales or purchase deals with related entities.
3. *Board positions:* Are relatives with no qualifications on the board? Are independent directors truly independent?
4. *Outside interests:* If promoters have significant stakes in companies other than the one under consideration, watch for conflicts of interest.
5. *Share pledges:* Promoters may take loans against pledged shares. A red flag as this means the promoters have already received monetary consideration in lieu of their shares and may be more likely to 'not care' what happens to the company.
6. *Preferential allotments:* Are promoters issuing shares to themselves at favourable prices?

If you notice any of these, the investment is likely junk, regardless of any short-term gains arising out of euphoria. As smart investors, we should steer clear of such traps.

Leverage

Leverage magnifies both gains and losses. Think of a business as a machine: you invest Rs 100 of your own capital, and it returns Rs 120. That's a 20 per cent return on your investment. Now, if you borrow Rs 50 from the bank, or your friend, at 10 per cent rate of interest to further invest, your total return magnifies to 30 per cent (that's Rs 20 of profit you previously earned less Rs 5 of interest you paid on the loan = Rs 15 total return on your own borrowing of Rs 50 that accounts for 30 per cent return), if the machine falters, returns drop dramatically. But you still have to pay the interest and principal amount on the loan without the business having returned that out of its profits. In the worst-case scenario, if the machine continues to falter, you will keep paying the interest on the loan without getting any profit in return from the business, forcing you to borrow more, further amplifying the impact.

This relates to both *investing in leveraged companies* and *your personal finances*. Leverage works well when things go as planned, but in unpredictable situations, like external shocks, it demands repayment regardless of cash flow. Should management focus on business strategy or debt repayment during tough times?

While debt is theoretically cheaper than equity as a source of finance for companies, high leverage can push companies to bankruptcy. Equity is considered expensive because investors expect a high return. But this is an 'expectation', not a promise. You would be happy with an 8 per cent FD but would scoff at a stock returning 8 per cent. Interest on debt on the other hand, while lower, is a 'promise'. It has to be paid, come what may, else borrowers go belly up. The optimal level of leverage is what a business can service even in the worst-case scenario—though predicting the worst is impossible. We've seen disasters like the 2008 financial crisis, the 2020 pandemic, and recent global conflicts. Low-leverage companies, generating enough cash flow without needing debt, are better positioned to weather these storms.

Arguments against low leverage include slower growth and potential management complacency. However, complacency can be tested through past behaviour and historical financial results. The same logic applies to personal finances: leverage can be useful when creating assets (e.g., a home loan), but harmful when used for consumption (e.g., a vacation loan).

In conclusion, it's not just the amount of leverage but how it's used. Sensible leverage creates long-term assets; bad leverage fuels consumption without future inflows.

Complicated Products

This book began by shunning complexity, and we're sticking with that. The 2008 sub-prime mortgage crisis showed us how dangerous complex products combined with leverage can be. Housing loans are simple: you borrow, buy a house and repay over time. But when complex features like giving loans without down payments, poor borrower screening and repackaging loans into risky investment products are added, it leads to disaster—just as it did in 2008 when housing prices surged, loans defaulted and the system collapsed.

Closer to home, we see complexity in products like insurance-as-investment schemes, fixed-return products with market-linked add-ons, and fancy sounding derivative strategies like iron condors and butterfly spreads. Complexity brings uncertainty, which swings your emotions and leads to bad decisions.

Simplicity, on the other hand, is steady and helps you sleep well at night. But it's boring. If a friend recommends an index fund, you might scoff at the lack of excitement. But if another friend boasts about making money trading options or benefiting from a gamma squeeze, you'll be intrigued. However, the simple index investor's net worth might surpass that of the trader, even if it doesn't sound as exciting. A recent study by SEBI revealed that 93 per cent of individual traders incurred losses in F&O between FY 22 and FY 24.[12] The aggregate losses surpassed

Rs 1.8 lac crore! On the other hand, a simple index fund or ETF would have mirrored the Nifty Index and compounded wealth. The Nifty 50 Total Return index has delivered a 15.63 per cent CAGR over the last fifteen years, 15.28 per cent CAGR over the last five years and 30.08 per cent over the last one year.

In reality, simplicity always trumps complexity—except when it comes to carbohydrates! Complex carbohydrates are good.

Valuation

You walk into an electronics store and find a great laptop with top-notch specs but which is out of your budget. There's another laptop with lower specs but within your budget. A week later, during Diwali, the higher-spec laptop is discounted by 50 per cent, making it as affordable as the lower-spec one. Easy choice, right? The specs didn't change, but the price did, so you'd naturally choose the better deal.

Now, apply the same logic to stocks. You identify a company with a solid business, strong management, low leverage and long-term resilience. But the stock is priced highly because others see the same value. Stock valuation is based on multiples of earnings, like P/E (price to earnings) or EV/EBITDA, but unlike a laptop, valuations of stocks fluctuate with market sentiment, narratives and emotional decision-making. This happens because:

- Price is very observable. But valuation is a moving target, based on a host of underlying factors.
- Stories and narratives distort emotions and induce people to take poor decisions by buying stocks at higher valuations.

The term *margin of safety* refers to buying at the right valuation, which often occurs during pessimistic periods when stock prices drop despite the company's strong fundamentals—just like the discounted laptop.

It takes time for value to kick-in. An FMCG stock became the butt of all memes when its price did not move. It was called the 'stable coin of Rs 200' when it languished at that price for two years. But the underlying business was growing. From March 2020 to March 2022, the share price did not move but the underlying business was still resilient. ROCE remained strong at around 30 per cent. Revenues increased by 20 per cent. Debt was very low. Profits and operating cash flows were stagnated but the business had the sheer platform and power to be able to grab opportunities in the future, courtesy strong capitalization with lower debt. The valuation from 2020 to 2022? A P/E of 13 to 15. The P/E today is around 26. Profits have gone up about 35 per cent but the share price has gone up more than double due to the P/E expansion. P/E expansion is nothing but the market offering a higher valuation multiple. It is a stage when broader participants recognize the value and swoop in to buy, driving the prices higher. Most wrong investment decisions are taken when valuations are high because investors don't want to miss the bus.

Let's look at an opposite example—a leading NBFC—the share price has not moved for the last three years trading at around Rs 7,000. The P/E in August 2021 was 83! You were paying 83 times earnings to buy the stock. That P/E has gone down to 32. Profits on the other hand have gone up from Rs 6,000 crore in 2021 to a staggering Rs 19,000 crore in 2024. An increase of 300 per cent! But the share price has not moved. That's because in 2021, it was trading at a high valuation and today, the valuation is only normalizing. (Owing to the peculiar nature of lending businesses, the price to book value i.e. P/B is a better metric than P/E. The P/B was at 12 in August 2021 and is now around 7. Once again, shouting out loud that investment returns are highly dependent on valuations.) Is this a bad business? I would go out on a limb and argue to the opposite effect. But is it a good investment? That depends on the valuation.

Colloquially asking 'is this stock good?' is actually meaningless. The question should rather be 'is this a good company whose stock is valued at a fair price?'.

And now that you have seen the four horsemen from both faculties, try to run away, far far away from all of them. Here is Morgan Housel's thought-provoking quote: 'Controlling your time is the highest dividend money pays.' And where would you rather use your time? Recouping lost progress (whether excess calories or excessive spending/bad investments) or being happy with less?

Here's a practical example of how using our simple mathematical calorie formulae can make us understand what not to do.

We learned about BMR in the opening chapter—the rate at which our body burns 70 per cent of calories at rest, doing absolutely nothing. But this BMR will keep dropping based on age and level of activity. What we physically work for are the remaining 20–30 per cent of the calories. This was a simple plan created for Mihir's friend, Raj, who wanted to lose weight. This plan has been made bearing in mind that he likes to occasionally indulge in sweet treats, and that not doing certain things is the key to his success rather than doing them.

Raj's current TEE is about 1,800 calories, so he will need to make a plan with fewer calories than this.

Particulars	Quantity	Carbs	Proteins	Fats	Total calories
Breakfast					
Black coffee/tea	1 cup	-	-	-	-
Whole eggs	2	5.0 g	12.0 g	10.0 g	138
Butter/ghee/oil	5 g	-	-	5.0 g	45
Cheese	1 cube	0.4 g	5.0 g	7.0 g	85
Breakfast total	-	**0.4 g**	**17.0 g**	**22.0 g**	**267.6**
Lunch					
Chapatis	2	30.0 g	6.0 g	1.6 g	158
Green sabji	1 cup	14.0 g	4.0 g	2.0 g	90
Butter/ghee/oil	5 g	-	-	5.0 g	45
Curd	100 g	4.0 g	4.0 g	3.0 g	59
Dal	1 bowl	29.0 g	11.0 g	5.0 g	205
Lunch total		**77.0 g**	**25.0 g**	**16.6 g**	**557.4**
Evening snack					
Black coffee/tea	1 cup	-	-	-	-
Protein shake in water	½ scoop	3 g	15 g	-	72
Peanuts	25 g	4 g	7 g	13 g	155
Evening snack total		**7.0 g**	**21.5 g**	**12.5 g**	**226.5**

Particulars	Quantity	Carbs	Proteins	Fats	Total calories
Dinner					
Paneer	100 g	1.0 g	19.0 g	27.0 g	323
Butter/ghee/oil	5 g	-	-	5.0 g	45
Rice	50 g	38.5 g	3.3 g	-	167
Dinner total		**39.5 g**	**22.3 g**	**32.0 g**	**535.2**
Grand total		**124 g**	**86 g**	**83 g**	**1,587**
Target (g)		120 g	105 g	75 g	1,575
Target (calories)		480	420	675	1,575
Target macro composition (per cent)		30	27	43	
Target achieved (per cent)		103	82	111	

Let's summarize what is happening with Raj's plan by breaking down the primary focus:

- Avoiding calorie-dense foods by focussing on natural foods that will satiate his appetite.
- Allocating macronutrients as per his target weight-loss goal.
- Keeping a small buffer of calories to ensure he can include cheat meals without compromising on his diet. Each meal has been prepared in such a way that there is protein and fibre to ensure that Raj meets his macros while also ensuring that he feels satiated after every meal. Carbohydrates, which are generally higher in calories per serving, are kept in

controlled quantities as Raj is the CEO of an investment management firm and gets decent movement, but not as much as an extremely active individual or athlete.

The buffer of 300 calories means Raj can indulge in a 100-calorie peda or any other type of sweet offered by colleagues or friends. The best part is that because he will be satiated with the natural foods, his body won't have the urge to indulge as much in these sweets as he would have if he had eaten them on an empty stomach.

If we continue to focus on the formulae from the first chapter and stick to quality foods, coupled with decent levels of exercise, there is a higher probability that we may not be pursued by the four horsemen.

As Morgan Housel writes, 'Engaging in exercise resembles having wealth. It involves resisting the temptation to indulge after hard work. True wealth lies in declining that indulgence and instead, burning more calories than consumed. This demands self-discipline.'[13]

Key Principles Learned from This Chapter

- Anything in excess is bad, whether in terms of nutrition or investing.
- Learning what not to do is arguably more important than learning what to do.

4

The Power of Compounding

As we begin this chapter, it would be great to remember the words of two twentieth-century figures.

Dean Acheson, the US Secretary of State under President Harry Truman just after World War II, said, 'Always remember that the future comes one day at a time.'[1]

Meanwhile, legendary physicist Albert Einstein said, 'Compound interest is the eighth wonder of the world. He who understands it, earns it; he who doesn't, pays it.'[2]

In the pursuit of both health and wealth, compounding operates as a force of exponential growth, where small actions or investments, consistently applied over time, yield significant and often transformative results.

But most people fail at grasping the essence of compounding, as it does not work in a linear fashion in the way most people think it does.

In this chapter, the goal is to explain how compounding works in long-term investing, the growth of great companies and the fittest individuals, and why all these people are some of the most boring you will ever meet.

The Power of Compounding

Author Mark Manson explains this non-linear process of compounding through the examples of American Navy SEAL training.[3] There's a part of the training called 'drown-proofing', where your hands are bound behind your back, feet tied together, and you are dumped into a nine-foot-deep pool. Your job is to survive for five minutes. Like most of SEAL training, the vast majority of cadets who attempt drown-proofing fail. Upon being tossed into the water, many of them panic and scream to be lifted back out.

But some people make it, and they do so because they understand two counterintuitive lessons:

1. The more you struggle to keep your head above water, the more likely you are to sink.
2. The more you panic, the more oxygen you will burn, and the more likely you are to fall unconscious and drown.

Understanding these paradoxical lessons is far more important than any cadet's ability to swim—it's more important than resilience, physical toughness, ambition, how smart they are, what school they went to, or how damn good they look in a crisp Italian suit.

This skill—the ability to let go of control when one wants it most—is one of the most important that anyone can develop. Not just for SEAL training; for life.

You see, for simple, mindless, repetitive tasks in life, effort and reward tend to have a linear relationship—the more time you spend in the car, the further you go.

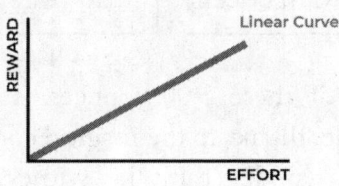

Source: MarkManson.Net

However, most activities in life are neither basic nor mindless. Most activities are complex, mentally and/or emotionally taxing and require adaptation. We don't always get what we put in. Over time, we get less.

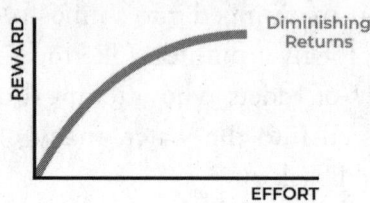

Source: MarkManson.Net[4]

Many a time, we have to push past plateaus and understand the reasons for those plateaus, so that we can grow beyond them.

Manson has explained this concept very aptly, and it is also applicable to the process of compounding.

If you've spent enough time on the internet, you've probably encountered the idea of compounding your wealth over decades of investing.

For those who are new to this, here's a brief overview of the simple process: invest Rs 5,000 a month at a rate of return of 12 per cent for a period of twenty years.

Monthly amount	Yearly rate of return	Time	Final amount
5,000	12 per cent	20 years	50,00,000

The journey of these 5,000 rupees is anything but easy though it is simple, thanks to the magical concept of compound interest. But its wonder can't be witnessed without going through periods of deep corrective phases.

The Power of Compounding

Here's a simplified explanation of the ebbs and flows that first investment of Rs 5,000 goes through. For the purpose of this exercise, we will only track the first instalment you pay.

In Year 1, you invest Rs 5,000 at a 12 per cent annual interest rate. You end up with Rs 5,600.

In Year 2, the Rs 5,600 from Year 1 earn 12 per cent, resulting in Rs 6,250.

This process continues, and by Year 5, your initial Rs 5,000 has grown to nearly Rs 15,000 thanks to the compounding effect.

However, in Year 6, you experience a significant drop in value, and your Rs 15,000 fall back to Rs 5,000, a 66.66 per cent decrease. This can be discouraging and might lead to doubts about investing.

Year 6 is a testing time for the investor, but also brings to the fore an important lesson about life—on every worthwhile journey, we go through harsh periods of downturn, and it is how we react to that situation that defines our success in the future. This is an oft-overlooked fact when it comes to compounding.

In Year 7, that Rs 5,000 grows by 60 per cent to Rs 8,000, and then in Year 8, by another 20 per cent to Rs 9,600.

If you have slowly and systematically invested Rs 5,000 every month, this compounding effect will lead to a final corpus of Rs 50 lakh.

Each instalment you invest travels through periods of ebbs and flows depending on when you have invested the money.

In simplistic terms, this is the power through which a boring process like SIP can allow you to swim with the tide.

The future is uncertain, but if you spend enough time being consistent, there is a high chance you can achieve your goal, and as you extend your time horizon, your probability of success keeps increasing.

It's essential to stay invested for the long term and not panic when you encounter temporary losses because, historically, the market tends to recover and grow over time.

Should you extend your holding period?
Increasing the holding period has historically improved chances of profitability, reduced drawdowns and lowered overall volatility.

	Holding period (in Nifty 50)				
	1 year	3-years	5-years	7-years	10-years
Probability of positive return (%)	70	85.4	93.9	94.8	99.7
Probability of negative return (%)	30	14.6	6.1	5.2	0.3
Worst scenario (%)	-55.7	-16.4	-6.6	-6.3	-1.6
Standard deviation	31	13.3	9.1	6.5	4.6

Backtest data of Nifty 50 data since inception   Source: Fisdom Research

Source: *LiveMint* personal finance[5]

This graphic by LiveMint, supported by data from Fisdom Research, shows how the probability of winning is not only about the power of compounding, but also about staying in the game for the long run.[6]

Notice the worst scenario is in Year 1. Very few investors would have stayed on after this year, but see how the probability of a loss drastically reduces after that year.

For the uninitiated, the term standard deviation refers to the volatility of returns—this reduces only with time.

Is long-term investing more profitable?
As you increase the holding period of the Nifty 50 index, data shows there is a greater likelihood of making higher returns.
(Returns in %)

	Holding period (in Nifty 50)				
	1 year	3-years	5-years	7-years	10-years
Probability 8% or greater return	56	59	62	73	76
Probability 10% or greater return	52	50	53	57	64
Probability 12% or greater return	48	42	39	42	51

Backtest data of Nifty 50 since inception   Source: Fisdom Research

Source: *LiveMint* personal finance

The Power of Compounding

Also, the longer you stay in the markets, the higher your chances of making that 10 per cent return.

The famous 'multibagger' stocks that individuals often dream about go through much longer periods of volatility compared to the example of the overall market above.

Here are examples of two actual stocks over a fifteen-year period from June 2007 to June 2022 that highlight the non-linear nature of compounding. We will refer to these stocks as A and B and not disclose names—potential sherlocks are free to run the numbers to identify them. These two, like every other big winner in the market, have gone through a similar cycle in the journey of compounding.

Measure	Stock A	Stock B
Holding period (years)	8.5	13.7
Trading days	2,724	3,586
Total gain	**1,270 per cent**	**8,890 per cent**
90 per cent of total gains in number of days	35	58
No. of days with 5 per cent or more gain	44	83
Percentage of trading days with 5 per cent or more gain	1.6	2.3
Days of price decline	**1,293**	**1,685**
Percentage of trading days when price declined	47	47

Source: Recreated from Pulak Prasad's *What I Learned About Investing from Darwin*.[7]

Observe from the chart: 35 days accounted for 90 per cent of the total gains made for Stock A, and 1.6 per cent of the trading days were days with gains of 5 per cent or more.

For Stock B, 58 days accounted for 90 per cent of the total gains, and 2.3 per cent of the trading days were days with gains of 5 per cent or more.

The point of this data is to show that the majority of returns for these two stocks came from a small number of trading days, and it's impossible to predict when these days will occur without staying invested.

Rather than focussing on the flashy total gains figure, observe the number of days of price decline that we would have to live through to achieve those staggering returns. Most investors don't have the stomach to work past these bad days.

Charlie Munger says individuals who don't have the stomach to lose 50 per cent of their capital on a given day will never reap the rewards the stock markets have to offer.[8]

I (Ankush) interviewed Sahil Kapoor, a peer who works in the asset management industry and is a disciple of health and fitness. I was drawn to the valuable insights he shares on markets and health on Twitter (X)—he embodies the principles of discipline and consistency in his investment philosophy and approach to work, and applies similar habits to his health routines.

Kapoor explains his views on the process of compounding by drawing on the theory of evolution, and mentions that compounding involves days with sudden leaps in progress, but one must endure the boring and stagnant phases for years. This phenomenon can be explained through a concept in evolution known as punctuated equilibrium, which suggests that most species remain unchanged for millions of years, followed by rapid periods of change, leading to the emergence of new species.

The Power of Compounding

Similarly, adopting high-performance habits and repeating them leads to results in a form of punctuated equilibrium. The outcomes can be non-linear, occurring either early or late. This means our actions guarantee results, but not the exact timing of their fruition.

Kapoor epitomizes repetition; he can perform any task over and over again continuously, and that's what's required in the never-ending world of our jobs, workout routines or investment processes. He emphasizes doing things 'without the expectation of closure'.

His concept of repetition involves creating an ongoing series of actions over an extended, indefinite period—a state of perpetual preparedness. He believes in always being ready, rather than getting ready.

Another analogy from the theory of evolution Kapoor uses is that compounding is nature's fundamental process. A cell self-replicates, eventually forming a complete organism without a blueprint. The cumulative effect of these cells results in the emergent property of life, where the sum of all vital organs and processes is greater than the individual parts. This is life; this is compounding—an unpredictable convergence of tiny, repetitive and persistent self-replicating wonders.

Any strategy, whether it's an investment plan, a nutrition plan or a fitness plan, will experience periods of downturn due to the vagaries of life, such as being busy at work, not having enough money to allocate, or even injury, sickness or simple lack of motivation. The key is to acknowledge that these vagaries will be a part and parcel of the journey, so that we can maintain consistency.

Rather than just starting an activity you want to commit to, it is better to approach it through the steps of Kaizen, the Japanese method of slow and continuous improvement. Here's how.[9]

Ask Small Questions

What is an exercise routine that I enjoy, and what do I need to do?

Do I have a goal in mind when investing, and how much do I need to keep?

Think Small Thoughts

I would like to start by running one kilometre at my own pace.

I would like to start investing Rs 1,000 in a basic fund to get myself started.

Take Small Actions

I will reach the park, and then things will fall into place.

I will open my account, set it up, and then decide on how I want to progress.

Solve Small Problems

I would like to stop panting while running.

I would like to not worry about the money I invest today.

Give Yourself Small Rewards

Today, if I can run a kilometre without stopping, I will reward myself with an ice cream.

As I reach a corpus goal of Rs 50,000, I will reward myself with some shopping.

Recognize Small Moments

I acknowledge how far I have come; I can now run five kilometres when I couldn't even run one just three months ago.

I acknowledge how much money I have saved when earlier I didn't even know how to start.

The Power of Compounding

Next, we need to choose a task that falls within the optimal range of difficulty—neither too hard nor too easy.

Getting into a state of flow requires engaging in activities at an optimal level of difficulty. The task should challenge us but not overwhelm us, nor should it be so easy that we get bored.

This chart by late Hungarian-American psychologist Mihaly Csikszentmihalyi shows that to maintaining consistency with an activity, we should find a path within this 'flow channel' that ensures we are motivated to do it without feeling overwhelmed.[10]

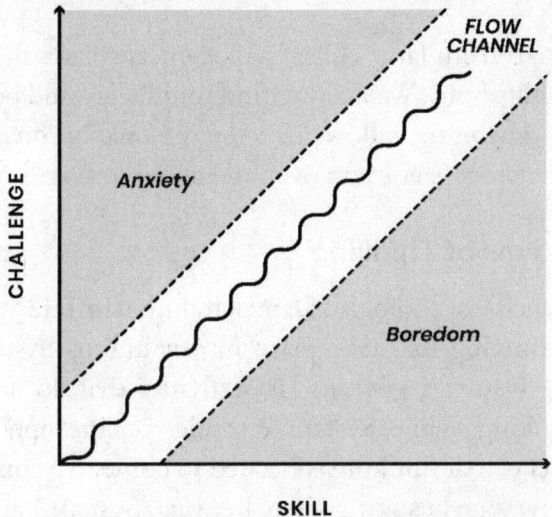

Source: Recreated image, inspired by Mihaly Csikszentmihalyi.

An activity becomes sustainable when we enter a flow state. It then becomes enjoyable.

Too much difficulty can lead to exhaustion and disruption of the rhythm. Consistency is paramount but one can't be consistent if they are pushing at 100 per cent on a daily basis.

Growth cannot be forced. As Warren Buffet says, 'You can't make a baby in one month by getting nine women pregnant.'[11]

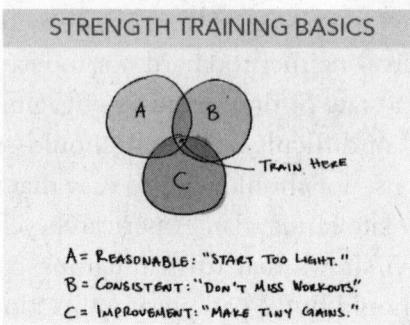

Source: Jamesclear.com

This chart from James Clear's blog encapsulates the strength training philosophy. We need to find middle ground between A, B and C—a habit that allows us to be reasonably consistent. We believe this process goes on over and above strength training.

Two Systems of Thinking

Renowned psychologist Daniel Kahneman referred to two types of thinking that take place in our brain—System 1 and System 2. System 1 governs fast activities that do not require much thinking, while System 2 resides on the opposite side, where intellectual thinking is needed to come to a conclusion.[12]

The flow state lies somewhere between System 1 and System 2, but the problem is that people spend too much time wavering in System 2 without taking quick actions.

The System 1 part of our brain is enhanced over time by setting up automated processes and systems.

System 2 is essential for making important big decisions in life, but we tend to overthink and procrastinate with simple habits such as setting up a process for SIP, paying insurance premiums, or going for a short workout, because we don't spend enough time setting up a process that allows us to easily take action.

In psychology, this concept is often referred to as the Goldilocks rule, which involves performing tasks at a 'just manageable' difficulty level. The human brain thrives on challenges, but only within an optimal range of difficulty.

This is why most people burn out in the workplace when they bite off more than they can chew in the hope of growth; companies fail when they aim to grow too fast and are not able to sustain it; individuals fail when they push their body too hard in the hope of getting stronger and faster within a stipulated time.

If growth could be rushed and sustained over long periods of time, most people would be successful. But it is not possible. It is a slow, boring journey, and hence most people fail when they attempt to fast-track results.

Even in the fitness world, there is a craze that a good workout is one that gets the heart-rate pumping and leaves us feeling gassed at the end. This is not the case.

When we place pressure on the body, it will find a way to adapt, or it'll get damaged. The only way to continually make it stronger and build muscle is by gradually increasing the intensity of the load, so that our body can recover better the next time. If we push the body too fast to achieve a goal, it will adapt by the process of inflammation, injury and stress.

Jim Collins, in his book *How the Mighty Fall*, took the example of Hewlett Packard (HP) to explain that a company is more likely to die of 'indigestion' from too much opportunity than 'starvation' from too little—HP bit off more than it could chew in the hopes of growing its company during the dotcom boom.[13]

Sanjay Bakshi, a famous Indian investor and teacher, has a great way of defining this. 'In equity investing, measure returns per unit of stress,' he says.[14]

Morgan Housel, in his book *Same As Ever*, mentioned how tree saplings spend their early decades under the shade of their mother's canopy.[15] A limited amount of sunlight means that the tree can grow only at a limited pace. But if we plant the tree in an open field and allow it access to unlimited sunlight, then the tree grows much faster, free from any shade. This fast growth means that the tree never had enough time to get dense. A tree that grows this quickly rots even quicker and never has a chance to grow old.

Housel also speaks about two identical baby fish—when we put one in cold water and the other in warm water, the first will grow slower than normal while the second will grow faster.

Now put these two fish back in room temperature water, and they eventually converge to become normal, full-size adults. The fascinating part is that the fish with slowed-down growth in its early days (cold water) goes on to live 30 per cent longer than the average, while the one in the warm water, which grew much faster, dies earlier than average.

Ernest Hemingway had a great method of being consistent with his writing—he said he would always write at 80 per cent intensity so as to not suffer from any kind of anxiety or burn out on arriving for the next day of writing.

He would always end a writing session only when he knew what came next in the story. Instead of exhausting every bit of energy and all ideas, he would stop when the next plot point became clear. This meant that the next time he sat down to work on his story, he knew exactly where to start. He built himself a bridge to the next day, using today's energy and momentum to fuel tomorrow's writing.

This is popularly referred to as the Hemingway Bridge, which would eventually compound into a large volume of work.

Ankush and His Dad's Story

I (Ankush) have observed that compounding is a byproduct of creating momentum—in my case, for example, writing and weightlifting are now parts of a daily routine because I simply show up every day even when I have no intention to do so.

Writing this chapter too, there were many occasions when I didn't feel like doing it, but I set a specific time to sit down and write before going to work every single day, and eventually, the ideas started flowing as fingers met the keyboard. Eventually, it has compounded into this book—it is not a culmination of a few sessions of writing, but rather of small sprints over a long time, as it is with any body of work you want to complete.

Brad Isaac, a young comedian, once asked the legendary Jerry Seinfeld what his secret to success was, and recounted the answer.[16]

'He said the way to be a better comic was to create better jokes, and the way to create better jokes was to write every day. He told me to get a big wall calendar that has a whole year on one page and hang it on a prominent wall. The next step was to get a big red magic marker. He said for each day that I do my task of writing, I get to put a big red X over that day.

After a few days, you'll have a chain. Just keep at it and the chain will grow longer every day. You'll like seeing that chain, especially when you get a few weeks under your belt. Your only job is to not break the chain.'

Seinfeld was not banking on motivation but on consistency to fuel his creative spark.'

My father, Ajit Datar, follows an exercise regimen built on this 'Seinfeld method'. He has a calendar set up in his room on which he ticks off each day that he exercises. He is a diabetic and a heart patient, who began his journey to health by joining a gym in February 2022. This is a picture of the calendar page for March 2022.

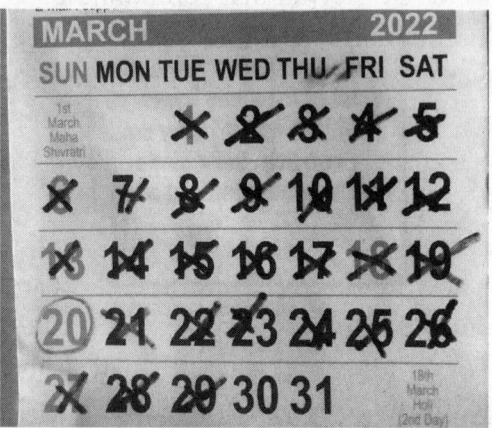

Just look at his progress. He was sixty-two years old at the time. It just goes to show it's never too late to start.

This is a picture of him on day one—he had never worked out in the gym, could barely squat, and couldn't sit cross-legged.

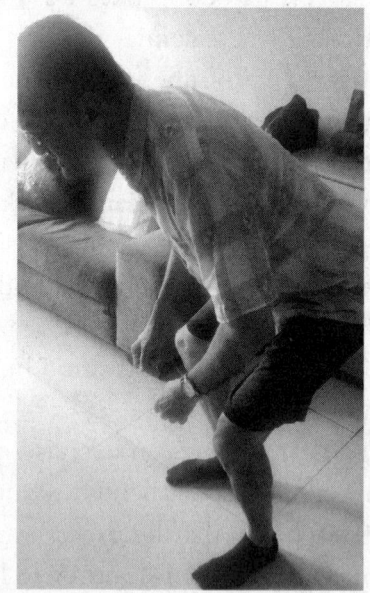

He progressed slowly, and by the thirtieth day, you can see him getting there with freehand full-range squats.

Today, at age sixty-four, he easily pulls off barbell squats, and can now sit cross-legged.

My father is applying the same principles we spoke about in this chapter.

1. If you're serious about progressing in your fitness journey, you need to keep track of your lifts and reps. Making notes from your previous sessions is the only way to strengthen progressively.
2. Drop your ego and focus on the form of your sets to ensure maximum muscle gain, which comes from contracting the muscle completely to failure.
3. Make a schedule to ensure you know what you must do once you arrive at the gym.

   Here is my father's schedule:

   Monday: Push day
   Tuesday: Stretching + walking
   Wednesday: Leg day
   Thursday: Free weights
   Friday: Pull day
   Saturday: Stretching + mobility at home
   Sunday: Brisk walk

   Of course, you can—and should—customize it to your preference.
4. As cliché as it may sound, showing up is the most challenging part of the process, and just by doing that, you can complete 90 per cent of your task.

My father's miraculous story was possible only through the Kaizen method, asking himself the basic questions about what he wants from this activity.

The mere repetition of a behaviour causes our nervous system to believe that the specific actions involved, and the context in which they are embedded, are important. This could be for good or bad. Choose what you repeat wisely.

Tied in with consistency are two related concepts: 'small incremental improvement' and 'progressive overload'. Motivational literature is filled with stories and anecdotes about both these concepts.

Small Incremental Improvement

Small incremental steps taken consistently and relentlessly can lead to massive exponential improvement.

In his book *Outliers*, Malcolm Gladwell describes how the Beatles tweaked and honed their skills by playing for long hours, seven days a week, for months in Hamburg, before they came to be the legendary band they are universally recognized as.[17]

Gladwell has also highlighted the constant tinkering and incremental changes that preceded the launch of the Apple iPhone. Apple's current market capitalization and phenomenal success are a consequence of a long period of relentless refinement by its engineers, harnessing years and years of compounding.[18]

Jim Collins, in his book *Good to Great*, explains a similar concept for all companies that have gone from being good to great by harnessing the power of compounding, through his example of the flywheel effect.[19]

'Picture a huge, heavy flywheel—a massive metal disk mounted horizontally on an axle about thirty feet in diameter, two feet thick and weighing 5,000 pounds. Your task is to get this massive flywheel to rotate as long and as fast as possible,' he writes.

'You push and push, as the flywheel keeps moving slowly, barely by half an inch or so. After two to three hours, the flywheel moves one turn. You keep pushing for seven, eight, nine, ten, fifty, a hundred hours while the flywheel gains momentum, and then *boom,* suddenly the flywheel is moving with great ease after the two-hundredth hour of pushing, and now it is getting easier to push the flywheel as it has picked up significant momentum.

If you asked the person pushing the flywheel what was that one big push that caused this thing to go so fast, the person will tell you it was the cumulative effort of all the pushing, not just that one push.

Good-to-great transformations never happen in one fell swoop.'

In fact, Collins was often asked by his fellow researchers who would interview companies during the background work for this book, 'Do we have to keep asking that stupid question about commitment, alignment and how they managed change?' Collins replied, 'That's not a stupid question, it's one of the most important.'

Another team member said, 'Well, a lot of executives who changed companies think it is a stupid question. Some don't even understand the question!'

Collins responded, 'Yes, we need to keep asking it, we need to be consistent across interviews. Besides, it's even more interesting when they don't understand the question because it allows us to understand how the company overcame resistance to change.'

For good companies that stick to a consistent plan of action, problems like motivation and commitment just melt away. They largely take care of themselves.

James Clear, in his book *Atomic Habits,* speaks about an ice cube in a room.[20] It sits there and nothing happens. You raise the temperature by one degree, and still nothing happens. Another degree, nothing happens; another degree and absolutely nothing has happened. But all it takes is one degree above freezing point for it to melt. We should keep this analogy in mind and not expect our ice cubes to melt immediately after changing the temperature by a degree or two; we need to go degree by degree, maintaining steady habits to achieve change.

This same phenomenon ties back to Sahil Kapoor's example of sudden spurts in the process of compounding when investing our money in the markets.

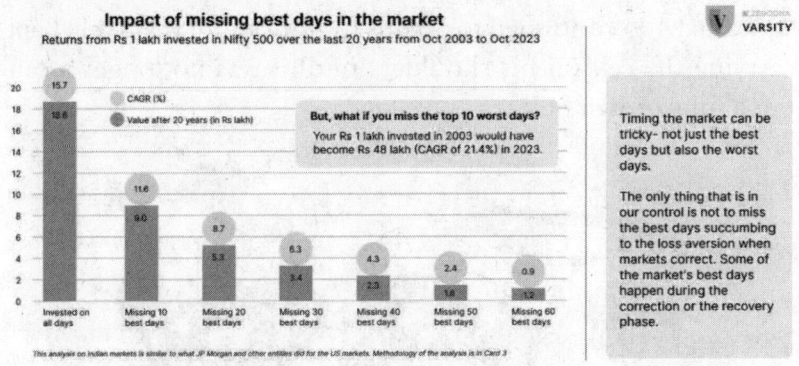

Source: Zerodha Varsity

Research by Zerodha Varsity highlights the fact that most of the value earned in the process of compounding is from sudden spurts during the best days of the market.[21]

'What appears to be a rapid shift is often preceded by a gradual process. Our results gradually explode or vanish thanks to the small habits we repeat each day.

What radical change are you slowly marching toward? An incremental explosion or an incremental vanishing?' as Clear wrote.

Case in point: a Chinese bamboo tree takes more than five years to start growing, but once it starts, it grows rapidly to a height of eighty feet in less than six weeks.

Progressive Overload

This is the next step—it refers to the gradual increase in the intensity or difficulty of a task. It's a step one should proceed with once consistency has been set in motion.

This is well illustrated by a story that is told about Milo of Croton, a fabled wrestler and strongman of ancient Greece who was said to carry a bull on his shoulders. How did he do it?

One day, a calf was born near Milo's home. He decided to lift the small animal and carry it on his shoulders. The next day, he returned and did the same, and then again the next day, and so forth. Milo continued to do this for four more years. He kept carrying the calf on his shoulders until it was no longer a calf but a fully grown bull.

Source: Greek Reporter[22]

My dad thought of the nifty idea of buying 0.5 kg dumbbell plates to aid in his progression. These tiny weights make a crucial difference when a heavy weight category is reached, where the increase in reps and weights is much slower. They also keep one's ego in check. Most people in the gym will progress with weights of five to ten kilos per set, but logically this makes no sense. If it worked then within a year, a human being would be able to lift a car.

I (Ankush) use this rule of consistency and progression with long-distance running too. When we first start running, we should have a modest goal in mind. Gradually, we should extend that distance a wee bit further. We cannot expect to run a full marathon the first time we step out. However, with incremental extensions, we will get there.

When it comes to investing through SIPs into equities, we can follow the same rule—investing every month on a specified day. The investment can be automated and can happen regardless of whether the world is ending or not, because the goal we have set has conditioned us in a way that uncertainties in life will keep happening, but our process will allow us to get past them.

Let us say appraisal season rolls around and your monthly salary now goes up by 10 per cent. So, you now have Rs 500 more to invest along with the Rs 5,000 in our initial example at the beginning of this chapter. It is prudent to now start deploying Rs 5,500 per month, and so on, till the day you retire. It is really that easy, but something that most people fail to grasp due to the illusive nature of the stock markets.

I (Ankush) came across a fascinating example of how consistency in the process, and not 'chasing' the best returns every single time, is the key to excellent returns in the long term—from legendary investor Howard Marks' investor letter of September 2023.[23]

Marks' friend, Dave VanBenschoten, who manages a pension fund, told him that in his fourteen years in the job, the fund's return had never ranked above the twenty-seventh percentile or below the forty-seventh percentile of the pension fund universe.

But these average rankings over fourteen years put the fund in the top 4 per cent returns performance because most funds shot themselves in the foot trying to chase returns without adhering to a defined process.

Let's hear again from the most successful investor ever, Warren Buffett, who said we don't have to be smarter than the rest; we have to be more disciplined.[24]

William Green's book *Richer, Wiser, Happier* presents brilliant insights drawn from interviews with some of the world's most successful investors.[25]

A master investor covered in this book is Tom Gayner, the CEO of Markel Corporation. Gayner manages close to US$20 billion in stocks and bonds, a collection of nineteen fully owned companies and around 17,000 employees.

Gayner once weighed more than 200 pounds, and proclaimed to his friends that he would lose one pound per year for ten years. That sounds like a ridiculously small number, but that's where the power of compounding comes into play.

'If you're an executive or a money manager who has these kinds of responsibilities, you're playing the game 24x7. There are no days off. As a consequence, I think it's very important to be disciplined about paying attention to your wellness, your exercise, work-life balance—all these sorts of things. Such behaviour may not create the outcome that you want, but it improves your odds,' Gayner is quoted as saying.

Gayner was once on an airplane when he came across a news article with the headline, 'Do you hate running?' He did hate it, so he read the article, which laid out a twenty-eight-day programme that began with running a maximum of five minutes per day.

This grew to ten minutes, then twenty, and so on. He now runs five times a week and has continued this habit for the last five years. Green describes him as someone who likes to be 'directionally correct'.

When Green visited Gayner in New York, the lunches and dinners consisted of Caesar salads, fish and Brussels sprouts, topped off with ice cream.

Gayner states that if one wants to be consistent, the key is to be 'radically moderate' and not be an extremist.

The author had interviewed Gayner in 2017, when he weighed 194 pounds. In 2020, Gayner informed Green that he now weighed 189 pounds. While this may sound like a low number to lose, Gayner thought of it as a significant figure since this had been his weight nearly thirty years ago. He was able to get there just by aiming to reduce a small number of pounds in an achievable and sustainable manner.

He used the same approach in his investing. Unlike yo-yo dieters who move from one fad diet to the next, or investors who keep shifting from one short-term bet to another promising strategy, he places his focus on a strong process which involves ticking four boxes and investing ideally with a 'forever time horizon'.

1. The business must be profitable, with good return on capital and not much debt.
2. The management team must have equal measures of talent and integrity.
3. The company should have ample opportunities to reinvest its profits at handsome rates of return.
4. The stock must be available at a 'reasonable' price.

The conclusion we can draw from Gayner's account is that 'resounding victories tend to be the result of small, incremental advances and improvements sustained over long stretches of time'.

From 1990 to 2019, Gayner's stock portfolio achieved an average annualized return of 12.5 per cent as against the 11.4 per cent for the S&P500—that means if one had invested $1 million with Gayner in 1990, the portfolio would be worth $34.2 million in 2019, as against $25.5 million if one had invested in the S&P500.

This was a great example of lateral thinking, using the principles of one discipline and applying it to another. Gayner found his sweet spot.

What is resounding about this strategy is the intentionally slow rate at which Gayner wanted to lose weight over the years by just sticking to a process—most people would aim to lose twenty pounds in a year only to fail miserably and fall into an endless cycle.

I (Ankush) quite resonate with Gaynor's account of my own running journey twelve years ago. It started in 2011 when I wanted to shed some extra kilos I had put on which made me look round. I started running in a nearby park with the intention to just lose some weight and eventually stop. I would run and run till I got tired. From twenty minutes non-stop to thirty minutes, and then eventually three hours of non-stop running at a stretch. This journey of becoming a marathon runner was one which took me years, to get to by aiming to just add a few minutes or a little bit of pace on every run and not being dejected when I achieved neither during runs.

Now whenever I take a break from running I know my pace and stamina will drop off but knowing how long the process takes, I never rush to increase my stamina or pace, I aim to increase either of the two at a slow pace by just being consistent by accepting what my body is capable of.

I use the same principle with my weight-lifting progress, every day I come to the gym I aim to do 1 rep or 1 pound more. I can confidently say after five years of following this process that most 99 per cent of people in the gym cannot lift the weights I do and there is no magic in my process.

Bench Press Progress		
Week	**Weight**	**Repetitions**
Week 1	35 kgs	5,5,4,3
Week 2	35.5 kgs	4,4,4,3
Week 3	36 kgs	5,3,4,3
Week 4	36 kgs	5,3,4,3
Week 5	36 kgs	5,4,4,3
Week 6	37 kgs	3,3,2,3
Week 7	37 kgs	3,3,2,3
Week 8	37 kgs	4,3,3,3
Holiday + Minor-Injury Three-Week Break		
Week	**Weight**	**Repetitions**
Week 9	34 kgs	6,6,4,3
Week 10	34 kgs	6,4,4,3
Week 11	34 kgs	6,3,3,3
Week 12	35 kgs	4,3,3,3
Week 13	35 kgs	5,4,4,3
Week 14	35.5 kgs	4,3,3,3
Week 15	35.5 kgs	4,3,3,3
Week 16	36 kgs	4,3,3,2
Week 17	36 kgs	4,4,3,2
Week 18	36 kgs	5,4,4,3
Week 19	37 kgs	3,2,2,2
Week 20	37 kgs	4,4,3,3
Week 21	37.5 kgs	4,3,3,2
Week 22	37.5 kgs	4,4,4,4

It took me six months to go from a 35 kg bench press on each side to a 37.5 kg bench press on each side, however my strength and muscle saw significant development during this boring upmove of doing the same repetitive exercises day in and day out.

You will also be shocked as to how far you have come in your fitness and investing journey when you stick to a process.

Today my monthly SIPs are worth almost as much as my monthly salary when I first started working.

Today my bench pressing ability in the gym is five times more than it was five years ago simply because I stuck to a process.

As soon as we see a slight dip in energy, we seek a new strategy, even if the old one was still working. Machiavelli noted that 'men desire novelty to such an extent that those who are doing well wish for a change as much as those who are doing badly'.

This is why many of the most habit-forming products are those that provide continuous forms of novelty, such as video games, intra-day trading and junk food.

This high level of variance leads to the release of cheap dopamine. And, as we know by now, the danger is that we are always left craving more and more of that item and in different forms.

Dopamine will be covered in detail in the next chapter on information overload.

Look at the body of Arnold Schwarzenegger and the wealth of Warren Buffett—individuals who achieved the highest levels in the worlds of fitness and investing respectively. It's simple in theory—they found their circle of competence and continued doing the basics for years and years.

Both individuals were gifted with unique genetics too, but they did not waste them, and focussed on simple habits to maximize their potential.

Buffet didn't get carried away with any new styles of investing, just as Schwarzenegger didn't get carried away with new fads in the world of fitness. They survived for years and years following the same principles of compounding. They still preach the same principles in terms of picking out stocks or strength training. One is ninety-three and still going as the world's top investor; the other is seventy-five but one really can't tell he's that old.

What they both do is focus ruthlessly on what they are good at, making sacrifices by delaying gratification and believing in the power of compounding. They might be outliers of success in their fields, but with compounding, even an average Joe like us can find success.

Our goal should be to try to follow the processes of these individuals without falling prey to the envy of what they achieved, because the circumstances of everyone's life are different.

While boring repetitive tasks are important in the journey of compounding, it is essential that we are doing the right tasks. Else, we are incurring what is known as opportunity cost or sunk cost in the form of time wasted.

It is explained by the sunk-cost fallacy in psychology. A sunk cost is one that is incurred and cannot be recovered.

Our textbooks teach us about this cost in an economic sense, but it presents itself in real life too in the form of:

- Spending too much time on activities we may not particularly enjoy.
- Spending too much time on a relationship we are scared of losing.

- Investment in a stock or fund we become too emotionally attached to and hence hold on to, even though it is giving us no return.
- Doing a particular form of exercise or following a certain nutrition plan, even though neither of these processes are giving us the results we want.

This idea of holding on to a strategy for as long as possible or expecting something to be a winner leads to what is known as the 'endowment effect', which means that we tend to value something more than what it is actually worth. Hence, it's a sunk cost.

Reviewing one's process to ensure that we are on the right path to harness the power of compounding is important. Merely doing things for the sake of it over many, many years does not necessarily translate to the power of compounding.

There is a human tendency to hold on to things in which we have invested too much time or money, and we are scared of what may happen if we are faced with uncertainty over letting go.[26]

The same sneaky fallacy goes by another name—the 'Ikea effect'. You know that feeling when you assemble an Ikea set from scratch? Suddenly, it's the most valuable thing in your life!

It's not just about furniture. It's about the time and the effort you've invested. Driving to Ikea, buying it, hauling it home, and assembling it. You're emotionally invested now, and it's hard to let go.

This phenomenon extends to more than just flat-packed furniture—it's why we find it tough to cut ties with bad investments, failing projects, eating habits built across a lifetime, or even our relationships.

We've put time into them, so they must be worth it, right?

Recognizing when to let go can be the key to our success.

In the initial years, compounding tests our patience, and in later years, our bewilderment.[27]

As James Clear puts it, 'Our outcomes are a lagging measure of our habits. Our net worth is a lagging measure of our financial habits. Our knowledge is a lagging measure of our learning habits. Our health is a lagging measure of our eating habits. Our fitness is a lagging measure of our exercise habits.'[28]

I would like to leave you with an analogy:

'Your physique is like your net worth.

Good choices compound over time, bad choices also compound over time.

Most people are drowning in debt (body fat) with no assets (muscle) to go with it.'[29]

Key Principles Learned from This Chapter

- The power of compounding is not a flash in the pan. It is a culmination of years and years of being consistent with a process, be it in fitness, investing or relationships.
- It matters what we choose to be consistent with and not just doing something for the sake of compounding. Time is the enemy of bad habits and friend of good habits.
- The journey of compounding is not linear, it goes through multiple phases of disappointments. We need to get past these phases to enjoy its beauty.
- Great businesses, great relationships, great athletes—all these were built through years and years of doing the right things slowly, and brutally facing the facts.

5

Information Overload

'Nifty falls record 1,000 points in worst showing.'
'Dow falls 2,000 points, its worst day since Black Friday.'
'We are in for a deep, long recession.'
'Man dies in gym due to whey protein.'
'Man dies of heart attack in gym, is working out a cardiac risk?'

You probably read these headlines and think doom and gloom are on the horizon, but the fact is that isolated events create a distorted view of the world and cause panic.

It is called the isolation fallacy.

'Last year, 4.2 million babies died.' This awful number, seen in isolation, creates anxiety—4.2 million babies dying is a catastrophe.

But when put in the right perspective, the number is less disheartening. In the 1950s, this number was 14.4 million; in the 1980s, around ten million. The 4.2 million figure is from 2016. Today, that figure stands at 2.3 million.[1] Even a single baby dying is a heartrending tragedy, but improvements in healthcare and nutrition are reducing the number day by day. It gives us reason to hope for a day when the number will be zero, as it should be. But we may never get that perspective in a headline, because it won't catch our attention.

In 2016, a total of forty million commercial passenger flights landed safely at their destinations.

Ten landings ended in fatal accidents.

Of course, those are the ones that were covered on the front pages, because a safe landing is no news. Progress takes years, even decades, to acknowledge. A single event and one article on it can blow things out of proportion.

The point of this introduction is to tell you that headlines and news articles can paint a false picture for the reader.

Headlines are negative by design, to incite a reaction from us. If it can't do that, it hasn't done its job. With people's affinity towards shorter and shorter forms of content, it has become even easier to incite a negative reaction out of an individual.

Writer David Perell has explained how easy accessibility to information is becoming a double-edged sword, with two types of biases:[2]

Space Bias

A hundred years ago, our ideas and thoughts would have been shaped based on the place we were living in. Moving media was a difficult and expensive task, so information was restricted by geography and had to remain local.

Today, things are radically different. We live in an age of abundance. One scroll on Twitter and we can know the latest information about events in New York, Paris, London, Cape Town or Buenos Aires.

This is usually information relating to the previous twenty-four hours. This puts us in a day-long closed loop. Social media highlights ideas that are currently fashionable, rather than great time-tested ones.

Time Bias

The space bias leads to what is known as a 'time bias' or 'recency bias'. With old barriers broken and information more easily available, we are generally too focussed on the last few days or months and don't pay any attention to the last ten or hundred years.

With attention spans falling, few people have the patience or capacity for concentration to read and understand information in a more focussed manner.

Think of a 300-page book, as opposed to a 300-word news article. Every page in the book has been written with painstaking research and effort, with the expectation that it will be relevant over an extended period of time.

The news article breezily sets forth information that could be irrelevant in a few days. It is so much easier to read the news article.

When it comes to information on investing and health, it is much easier for the reader to get influenced by a single article or hack provided by someone on social media.

So, even though we are going through more information daily, it does not necessarily mean that we are more well-informed.

Rolf Dobelli traces the history of the newsletter in his book *Stop Reading the News*.[3]

Commercial newsletters first appeared around the year 1450, following the invention of the printing press. These newsletters were distributed through subscription models and were specifically tailored to meet the interests of wealthy merchants and financiers. They covered a wide range of topics, including political events, agricultural developments, local and international news, and provided detailed information on the schedules of merchant ships, cargo movements and other specialized subjects.

The origin of newspapers can be traced back to 1605 with the introduction of the weekly publication *Relation aller Furnemmen und gedenckwurdigen Historien* in Strasbourg, Germany. The popularity of newspapers quickly spread from Germany to Amsterdam, then to London, and eventually across Europe.

The first daily newspaper, *Einkommende Zeitungen*, was established in Leipzig, Germany, in 1650. In the following decades, the number of daily newspapers increased significantly across Europe, and eventually worldwide. Publishers began prioritizing content that could capture readers' attention and increase sales, regardless of its importance.

Back in the day, newspapers even highlighted on their front pages how smoking, or drinking cola, was a 'good thing'. Ask yourself what would be the equivalent of these trends today.

This trend of excessive information has been accentuated in the modern day with the birth of content creators.

Today, with the pace of artificial intelligence, new 'content' on health and investing is being dissipated on a daily basis. It is becoming an increasingly tougher skill for a beginner to understand what information is relevant.

Let's face it, there are only a handful of things that really matter when it comes to health and wealth, but the world of social media makes us overthink and complicate matters more than they already are, by providing us information every single day that makes us believe we could add another process to enhance our journey towards a healthier and more stable financial life.

There are two types of individuals who typically post information:

Finfluencers, who provide financial information for educational purposes.

Fitfluencers, who provide health information for educational purposes.

There are genuine influencers in these two categories who are looking to help individuals in their health and wealth journey by providing solid advice. In fact, I (Ankush) personally make sure I filter my socials to find these individuals, and have learnt a lot from them.

So where does the problem lie? It lies in those sets of influencers within these categories who tarnish this whole model of content creation by creating shortcut methods or sensationalist headlines to simply increase the number of followers or hack the algorithm to generate higher traction.

'5 ways to get shredded abs'

'3 simple ways to make $1 million and finally quit that job'

'Here are three stocks that you can invest in and forget about your job'

An average human would be easily attracted by these headlines because who doesn't want a fast-track way to achieve their dreams?

We tend to follow the herd on most occasions, and social media algorithms are tailor-made to get us to do that, in order to increase engagement.

Daily access to this form of information leaves us with a sense of false dreams.

The reality is that this leads to an endless vicious cycle. The individual realizes over the short term that these techniques are not working and moves on to the next method peddled by the next influencer. They haven't become millionaires, they haven't quit their jobs, they have failed to get that shredded six-pack, but they'll keep hunting for new shortcuts.

Some of these individuals even achieve the goals set out by the influencers, but then hit a roadblock—what's next? This is because they have been hyper-focussed on the goal and have not managed to enjoy the process.

Who is to blame? The consumer? The content creator? Both?

The content creator is choosing to engage the consumer because the latter is choosing to follow that content. The creator, seeing this trend, will start making more and more of that content without paying much heed to repercussions.

So, we must be conscious of the content we consume. There are some really good creators out there who have added tremendous value on the health and wealth fronts, but for every good one, there will always be another who uses negativity or sensationalism to draw our attention.

Consumers generally hate the good old 'boring' information on health and wealth, so creators will push more sensationalism to our timelines by hacking the algorithm.

In the past few decades, we have learnt to recognize the many hazards of poor nutrition: insulin resistance, obesity, heart disease and many more such issues.

We know that sugar and fast-food cause health issues and avoiding these is the first step to prevent these major diseases.

We know that trading in derivatives in the stock market causes most investors to lose money.

Despite this, why are most individuals addicted to these activities?

This addiction could be explained by a molecule in our brain called dopamine.

Focal Point of Our Health and Wealth Decisions

It is best to grasp the importance of dopamine before we progress further to understand how it plays the focal role in all the decisions we make in terms of our health and wealth. Dr Anna Lembke's book *Dopamine Nation* is an invaluable resource about this neurotransmitter.[4]

Dopamine communicates between nerve cells in the brain and is linked to mood, motivation, sleep, and many other functions in the body. It plays a bigger role in the motivation to earn the reward, than in the actual reward itself.

For example, the feeling before lighting that cigarette tends to release more dopamine than the actual act of smoking.

Same with the process of getting that early morning coffee, or even the feeling of buying a stock with the expectation of it going up by 1,000 per cent.

The feelings of pain and pleasure are found on overlapping parts of the brain through an opposite process mechanism, akin to a see-saw.

Source: Anna Lembke's *Dopamine Nation*.

The activities on the 'pain' side include exercising, eating healthy meals, taking up challenging tasks at work, continuing an investment process—essentially, difficult and boring tasks.

The activities on the 'pleasure side' include scrolling endlessly on social media, eating junk food, gambling in stocks—essentially, easy and thrilling tasks.

As we stated categorically earlier, we aren't soulless humans, and we believe many pleasurable activities should be done. But the human brain does not care about our views; it works on scientific facts.

Pleasurable activities release what is called 'cheap' dopamine.

As we do more activities that releases this, the see-saw of our brain starts tipping towards the pleasure side. In the course of that, an opposite act is taking place—what Lembke defines as 'gremlins' building up—on the other side of the see-saw.

The more we take part in cheap dopamine activities, the bigger and faster the gremlins are growing on the other end to tip the balance towards the pain side.

Source: Anna Lembke's *Dopamine Nation*.

Thus, with repeated exposure to pleasurable activities, we need more and more of the same activities to feel better.

This is why humans crave more of addictive substances—the more dopamine a drug releases and the faster it releases it, the more addictive the drug.

Some items high on the 'cheap dopamine' list are chocolate (55 per cent), nicotine (150 per cent), cocaine (225 per cent) and amphetamines (1,000 per cent).

Triggering cheap dopamine in today's world is super easy—we can drink, smoke, watch adult content, eat sugary foods, gamble in stocks, scroll on social media.

However, too much exposure to cheap dopamine-inducing activities can alter the brain and cause the formation of 'hippocampal tattoos', which can change our brain structure towards motivation for our entire lives.

To tip the scales of excess dopamine and maintain what is called 'homeostasis'—or equilibrium, for easier understanding—we need to counterbalance this by doing activities that challenge us and release dopamine in a much more gradual and sustained manner.

Working out, taking up challenging tasks at work or facing that problem that we have been running away from all help to release dopamine in a sustained quantity, and make us feel better.

This explains why when we ace a difficult exam, complete a difficult task at work, work out or do any activity that challenges us, dopamine release tends to be gradual and at a much higher rate that sustains for longer. We feel much better for longer when we do that one-hour gym session rather than sitting on the couch, munching fries and getting validated by the ten other folks who are doing the same thing.

We believe it's the same with investing in boring mutual funds for the long term, or holding on to a stock for many years through lull periods. It requires one to reprogramme their brains towards the pain side of dopamine, but as we know now, that leads to long-term rewards.

A study conducted in 2012 showed how dopamine released in professional equity market traders dictated the returns they generated.[5]

Those with a history of taking excessive risks and those who were too conservative had the worst results. Traders who were somewhere in the middle—the ones who were able to balance the risk efficiently—did the best. The study highlighted dopamine's role in accurately assessing risk and reward in trading.

I recollect when, back in 2014, I (Ankush) was looking out for internships in the financial markets and happened to get a meeting with a very respected and successful senior trader who built wealth by successfully trading for twenty years. He wanted to meet me in person and tell me to consider not taking up trading as a hobby or full time role, which made me think that he was probably doubting my abilities. He made me meet a senior trader who had quit his job at a big consultancy firm to become a trader at his office and allowed him to work there independently. The senior trader told me that he had been running losses on his proprietary trading for years but still continued to come back due to his addiction.

As I recollect my meeting with him ten years ago, I am grateful for that meeting with him to give me advice early on in my career and that he told me that he would be willing to give me the internship but it would not be a good decision.

Now don't misunderstand me, I personally know very successful traders who I respect and whom I would trust my money with but for me, it was a simple decision to avoid a game where the probabilities of not making money in the long term are higher than making more than investing in the fixed deposit of a bank.

Data does not lie; less than 1 per cent of traders in the markets are able to beat the returns of a bank fixed deposit.[6]

Even a genius like Isaac Newton fell for the greed of the stock market back in the day with the South Sea Bubble.[7]

In early August 1720, Newton found himself at a crossroads—during a year of unprecedented boom in London's stock market, he faced the decision of whether to sell off his remaining secure investments to acquire shares in the South Sea Company, a stock which had been rallying to high heavens on positive news. Since the beginning of the year, the firm, one of the largest private enterprises in history, had seen its shares soar eight times over, creating substantial wealth for countless investors. He couldn't escape the buzz of market speculation.

Typically a cautious investor, Newton had previously kept much of his wealth invested in dependable government bonds, which provided steady returns. While he did hold shares in a few prominent companies, including the South Sea Company, he was never known for actively trading on the market.

However, in recent months, Newton's approach had shifted. He had begun buying and selling more frequently, seemingly aiming to transform his sizeable fortune into an even greater one. By August, he had liquidated most of his bonds, exchanging them and other assets for South Sea shares. Now, he contemplated divesting the last of his bonds to acquire additional shares in the South Sea Company, which he did.

Ultimately, he chose to sell off nearly all of his bonds—a decision that would prove calamitous. Within a mere three weeks, the market took a sharp turn. By Christmas, it had collapsed entirely. Newton's losses, stated by many sources to have been around 20,000 pounds, would amount to millions of dollars in today's currency.

If we keep gobbling more and more of junk information, which is addictive just like junk food, once we try to go and detox, we'll find it difficult due to our body's new dopamine threshold.

Side-Effects of Junk News

Just like junk food, the side effects of excess consumption of junk news becomes apparent only after a while.

Speak to many great investors in the industry, and they will be more than happy that no one is talking about their investments. It means that when the stock does get discovered by the news, it would have already run up by a large margin.

Putting up information about strength training and eating a high-protein diet in the weekly health column is passé; it will not catch enough eyeballs.

Or see the pictures of many athletes' photos on the front cover of a newspaper or the net worth of the largest investors, no one will focus on the long process to reach that level for the athlete or the investor.

It's news when someone 'fit' gets a stroke. Unfit people get them every day, what's the novelty in that?

Remember this the next time you hear 'man dies of whey protein' or 'fit individual dies while cycling'.

It's designed to pique our interest.

Studies have shown, our central nervous system reacts strongly to sensationalist news and weakly to positive news or even that which requires some degree of interpretation.[8]

This is why it makes logical sense for someone who wants to bait or increase engagement on social media to share a polarizing view to trigger a response.

Negative information has twice the impact that positive information does.[9] In psychology, this is called negativity bias; in some cases, it is also labelled the 'loss aversion' bias.

I (Ankush) observe this phenomenon when I am speaking with clients too. I generally get a wary call from a client only if a stock is down 15 per cent than if a stock is up 150 per cent

Sensationalist negative news can create an unnecessary bout of stress in individuals.

Maintaining a healthy lifestyle demands willpower—the ability to think clearly, work efficiently, consume nutritious food and engage in physical activity.

As stress mounts, willpower diminishes.

We find ourselves trapped in a harmful cycle. Instead of going to the gym, we opt to browse through the news. We liquidate stocks or funds in our portfolio based on the belief that a particular war will adversely affect the economy.

This also leads to overconsumption of information. We tend to read more into things and assume that we know better.

In a popular study done in 1974, Paul Slovic tested the data of information overload on horse-race betting.[10] He gave an increasing number of data points about the horses to the people betting, then asked them not only which horse would win but also about the accuracy of their predictions. The result? The wealth of information had no impact on their accuracy, but just made them more overconfident.

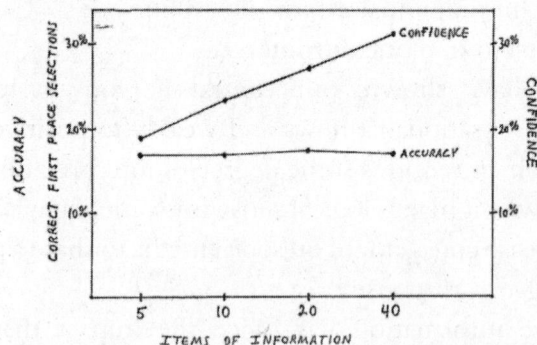

Source: Widmar and Hubbart, 'The perils of more data'.

Knowing more than required about a certain stock we want to invest in is not going to give us more of an edge; over-analysis leads to paralysis. Research has observed that the more frequently a person consumed different forms of media at the same time, the fewer brain cells there were in the anterior cingulate cortex—the part of the brain responsible for attention, moral deliberation and impulse control.[11] We will cover how this part of the brain plays a crucial role in our health and wealth decisions in a later chapter.

The more we scroll on social media and flick through information at a rapid pace, the more we encourage the formation of neuronal circuits adapted to the flood of information and multitasking.

This also happens to once-passionate bookworms who have been bit by the bug of social media scrolling—they are no longer able to read more than a few pages of a book.

Annie Duke explained this brilliantly in her book *Thinking in Bets*.[12]

This is how we think beliefs are formed:
1. We hear something.
2. We think about it, vet it, determining whether it is true or false.
3. We form a belief.

However, this is how people actually form abstract beliefs:
1. We hear something.
2. We believe it to be true.
3. Only later, if we have the time or inclination, we think about it and vet it, determining whether it is true or false.

Instead of altering our beliefs to fit new information, we do the opposite—alter our interpretation of that information to fit our beliefs. This explains how many people lose money on borrowed conviction without a financial adviser. Most get sucked into the hype cycle.

Similarly, most people get sucked into fad diets without taking the advice of a nutritionist.

This also leads to what is known as anchoring bias, a situation where we let a certain set of information anchor our beliefs, whether it is true or not.

We humans tend to believe that the information must be relevant, informed and well-reasoned.

Anchoring directly contributes to what is know as confirmation bias, where we assume that the decision we made is the best decision possible. We tend to look for data that supports our decision.

It becomes increasingly difficult for the consumer to filter out information when the smartest of minds start propagating ideas like cryptocurrencies, fad diets, get-rich-quick schemes.

Now we even have direct access to the thoughts of these individuals through social media, something that was not possible twenty years ago, so it has become easier for people to share information that could influence our decisions.

We saw this phenomenon play out in spectacular fashion from 2020 to 2022 with the rise of various cryptocurrencies being endorsed by some of the smartest minds in the world.

I (Ankush) even have clients in my professional line of work with years of investing experience to whom I advised not to invest in these currencies if they did not have deep knowledge on it, many of whom lost a lot of money on the same.

When we study history, we understand how this form of human behaviour has been going on for ages in different avatars, but social media has accentuated this trend at a rapid pace.

Morgan Housel writes that studying old newspapers is also a creative exercise to see how much of the news that was reported actually matters in today's age.[13]

'Every piece of financial information you read should be filtered by asking the question, "Will I still care about this in a year? Five years? Ten years?" The goal of information should be to help you make better decisions between now and the end of your ultimate goals. Read old news and you'll quickly see that life expectancy of your goals is higher than that of vast majority of headlines,' he writes.

Had you read this famous piece by *Business Week* published on 13 August 1979: 'To bring equities back to life now, secular inflation would have to be wrung out of the economy, and then accounting policies would have to be made more realistic and tax laws rewritten. For better or worse, the US economy probably has to regard the death of equities as a near-permanent condition—reversible some day, but not soon,' the piece stated.[14]

Housel points out if we had believed this article, we would have probably missed out on the huge stock market rally that followed right after.

A phenomenon called 'authority bias' makes people follow investors who have success and clout in the stock market. When other investors see headlines like 'famous investor XYZ buys a stake in ABC Engineers', they flock to the stock, completely disregarding their own asset allocation and goals. Such is the lure of the markets. That famous investor's goal and appetite to lose money on an investment would be completely different from ours.

This is a recipe for disaster that many retail investors fall for. To help counter this bias, there are two questions to ask:

'Have I done the work?'

'Have I independently verified everything?'

The same phenomenon takes place with the nutrition trends of famous athletes. If Virat Kohli has turned vegan and is being successful, people think it must be good. Or, if Michael

Phelps eats pizzas and ice creams while preparing for an event, it must be the way to go! A consumer who has spent no time in creating their own process will assume they should replicate these star athletes' eating habits because they look good and are successful.

Marketer Seth Godin explains how a novice sailor will focus on the winds and how they are constantly changing.[15] But an experienced sailor will focus on the currents, because even though the winds are always changing, the currents are persistent and even though they are invisible, a strong current can always overtake the winds. It is the same in investing. The stock price is clearly visible and a newbie investor tends to focus on only that without paying heed to the actual underlying business that is eventually going to be driving the stock price.

'The wind gets all the attention. The wind howls and the wind gusts ... But the wind is light. The current, on the other hand, is persistent and heavy. On a river, it's the current that will move the canoe far more than the wind will, but the wind grabs our attention ... [T]he wind is the breaking news of the moment, the latest social media sensation, and the cacophonous hype that surround us.'

They are engaging distractions, but our real work lies in understanding, mastering and harnessing the underlying currents to our advantage.

'It helps to see it first, and to ignore the wind when we can.'

So it is in the equity markets. Alarming headlines on the financial pages cause fear and panic in the minds of investors, and rightly so if the news outlets or social media are one's only avenues for gauging the stock market's performance. If you come across a headline 'Nifty falls 3 per cent, highest decline in twenty years' or 'S&P loses $7.4 trillion in this sell-off', the situation would obviously look scary.

But it should not be so when seen in the context of how much the value of the market has grown over the years. And we can do that by just zooming out.

From 1990 to 2022, the Indian and world markets have gone through tumultuous periods triggered by scams, economic downturns, changes in government and numerous other negative events. However, investors who have been able to stick through thick and thin have been rewarded. Investors in the equity market should expect to sail on choppy seas, but can equally expect to be well-rewarded for their fortitude and patience.

Pessimism sells; the optimist is made to look like a fool during downturns and lull periods.

The greatest investors in the Indian markets have sailed through the multiple periods of their portfolios being down 80 or 90 per cent to achieve the highs that they sit on today. I am sure they were laser-focussed on the underlying businesses and not paying too much attention to what headlines were telling them during the dotcom bubble, the 2008 crisis or the 2020 Covid-19 crash, to name a few events.

The perils of focussing too much time on events outside our control can be explained with the example of an archer getting prepared to fire her bow and arrow.

She can control which bow she chooses, which arrow she selects from her quiver, how far back she draws the bow and how still she holds it. But from the moment she lets the arrow fly, it's beyond her control. A gust of wind may knock the arrow of course, or it may break mid-flight. Something might get between the arrow and the target, or the target may move.

Almost all world events are out of our control, so don't waste too much time on them.

In his book *Fooled by Randomness*, Nassim Taleb says, 'Minimal exposure to the media should be a guiding principle for someone involved in decision making under uncertainty—including all participants in the financial markets.'[16]

In 1993, the internet carried 1 per cent of all communicable information. By 2007, its share was up to 97 per cent. Today, it carries virtually every piece of information.

Information overload is something that can get overwhelming and force us to do stupid things.[17]

Health is an excellent metaphor for this overload. David Perell explains how obesity rates and the number of people in incredible shape are both rising due to this overconsumption.

Through this graph, he explains that abundance of information is detrimental to the median set of consumers, but extremely good for a small number of conscious consumers who are able to efficiently filter out the noise.

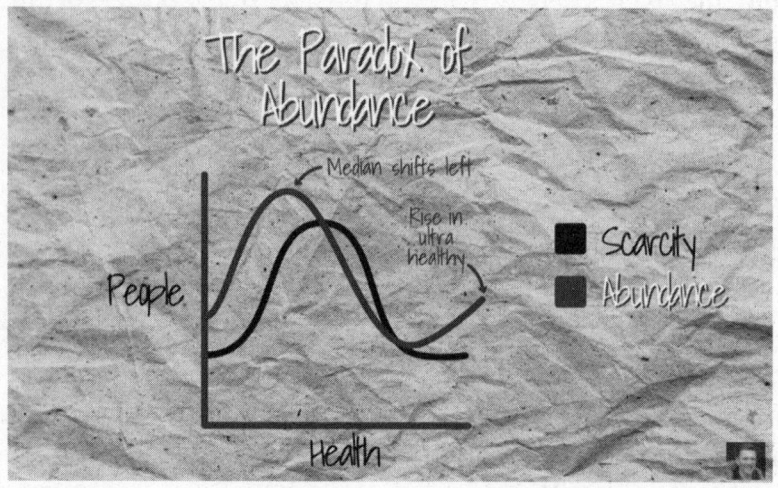

Source: David Perell, 'How to use your phone better than everyone else'.

Observe the black curve. In markets of scarcity, the median group does relatively better than when they have too much information, which is highlighted with the blue curve. Too much information actually shifts this graph to the left and causes more obese people.

Similarly, for conscious consumers, abundance of information actually leads to more healthy people as opposed to periods of scarce information. These people are able to filter out the unnecessary information and focus on what is important.

Books and long-form articles are like protein and fats: they are essential for maintaining and growing our body's muscle mass and for regulating hormonal functions.

News is like carbohydrates; one has to be extremely selective in what one consumes and the quantity one consumes. The news that is relevant to us may not be relevant to someone else.

Perell, who has influenced a large part of this chapter, highlights another important point on selective consumption of the news.[18] The news is just like cereal.

'Even though cereal is now viewed as over-processed and sugary, it was once viewed as a healthy food. Americans heard about the health benefits of cereal and ramped up their consumption. From the beginning, companies made heavy investments in advertising cereals because most people eat the same breakfast every day. Thus, just as readers are loyal to news sources, consumers are loyal to their favourite breakfast cereals. And like news, consumers inhale cereal during the frantic rush before work. Even if they aren't the healthiest options, they're cheap and easy to consume.'

In his book *Factfulness*, Hans Rosling asks the reader to imagine that we have a shield, or attention filter, between the world and our brain.[19] This attention filter protects us against the noise of the world; without it, we would constantly be bombarded with so much information we would be overloaded and paralysed.

Then, he asks the reader to imagine that the attention filter has ten holes in it—gap, negativity, straight line, etc.—that distort our perception of reality. Most information doesn't get through, but the holes do allow through information that appeals to our dramatic instincts. So, we end up paying attention to information that fits our dramatic instincts and ignoring information that does not.

Today, in the age of information overload and an abundance of tools to research, the ability to filter noise has become a superpower.

We would like to leave you with this beautiful quote from Pico Iyer's *The Art of Stillness*, 'As I came down from the mountain, I recalled how, not many years ago, it was access to information and movement that seemed our greatest luxury; nowadays it's often freedom from information, the chance to sit still, that feels like the ultimate prize. Stillness is not just an indulgence for those with enough resources—it's a necessity for anyone who wishes to gather less visible resources.'[20]

Key Principles Learned from This Chapter

- When it comes to health and wealth, don't get startled by headlines. Go deeper and try to make an independent judgement.
- When we set out to improve our health and wealth, to make sure we stay the course, we will have to learn how to completely ignore new information. This takes time and we learn with experience.
- Over-analysis leads to paralysis.
- With the wealth of information at hand, simplicity often seems underwhelming, when in fact it is the only thing that defines success in the longer term.

6

Don't Judge a Book by Its Cover

Almost everyone has heard of the old adage that makes up the title of this chapter, but how many of us actually implement learnings from it?

Nowhere is this truer than in the case of the food we put in our bodies. So many of us read the front of the packaging and see phrases like 'low in fat', 'no added sugar', 'high in vitamins' or '100 per cent fat-free', and assume the food is healthy.

When was the last time you turned the product around to understand the contents listed at the back of the packaging? What did you observe? If you have never engaged in this one-minute activity due to your busy schedule or stressful life, then this chapter is for you.

We assume what we see on the front of the label is the absolute truth because no one taught us from childhood or in school what these labels meant, and we weren't willing to dig deeper. But whether we're talking about nutrition labels or financial statements, there are two key principles to live by:

1. Don't judge a book by its cover.
2. If you don't understand it, don't waste your time over it.

Now that we have learnt in previous chapters about the basics of calories, it's time to look beyond the calorie count and delve deeper into the actual contents of the products.

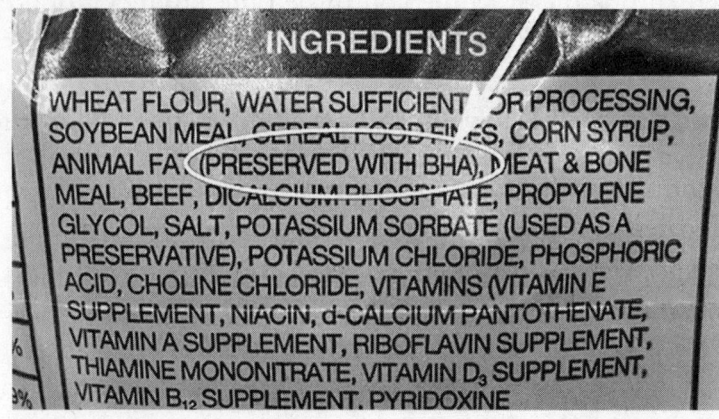

Take a look at this picture. Is the information provided enough to make a decision to buy the product?

Conventional wisdom would say this is a fairly low-calorie product with zero cholesterol, so it looks good enough to purchase. But we're missing the bigger picture. Let's dive deeper into the actual ingredients to get a better idea.

Note that 'BHT' has been added to 'preserve freshness'. A quick internet search will show that BHT is butylated hydroxytoluene with the chemical formula $C_{15}H_{24}O$. Since we are not chemists, we decided to check what it is used for.

Both BHT and a related compound BHA (butylated hydroxyanisole) are used to prevent fats from becoming rancid; BHT is used to preserve the colour, odour and flavour of food. It is found in many packaged foods and is directly added to shortening, cereals and other foods linked to fat and oil.[2]

What could be the possible side effects? Independent researchers have shown that the derivatives of BHA and BHT, called metabolites, may contribute to carcinogenicity or tumorigenicity.[3] Some independent researchers have even found there could be individuals who may not be able to metabolize BHT and BHA efficiently, resulting in health and behaviour changes.

With this new knowledge, let us ask ourselves if this item is worth consuming on a daily basis, or providing to our children regularly. Shouldn't we try our best to avoid foods made in a chemistry lab, which we can't even pronounce? We don't even need to do due diligence on the other artificial ingredients, considering how bad BHT itself is.

Focussing solely on the calorie count and not considering the actual contents of the food can be hazardous. Natural and healthy foods typically have naturally occurring ingredients.

Now, let's compare the previous label with that of a food item with a higher calorie content.

energy	235.0 kcal
protein	12.0g
carbohydrate	21.2g
added sugar	0.0g
natural sugar	14.6g
fat	11.4g
trans fat	0.0g
MUFA + PUFA	8.3g

Source: The Whole Truth Protein Bar

Two hundred and thirty five calories per serving, so does that make the product more fattening? By now, we have learnt the basics of 'calories in and calories out', and we know this is not true.

Now let's have a look at the ingredients at the back of this high-calorie food:

cashews	34%
cranberries	21%
dates	19%
raw whey protein	17%
cocoa butter	5%
almonds	4%

Observe the number of ingredients being used—the fewer there are, the simpler the product, and the higher our chances of understanding the benefits of the food and grasping the macro and micro-nutrient profiles in our allocation of daily calories. We barely need to research what each ingredient means.

However, the durability of this product would be much lower than traditional processed food because it does not contain a long list of chemical additives to preserve the shelf-life.

While focussing solely on calories, which is a short-term metric and is also important, we are losing sight of the bigger picture—the nutritional value of the underlying ingredients that are going to drive our long-term health.

The information on the back of the label should be what guides the consumer's choice; the front is only there to dazzle.

The truth of a food product is regulated by a governing body called the Food Safety and Standards Authority of India (FSSAI) in this country, or an equivalent body in others. This regulator lays the ground rules for the information on the label.

Now, with this basic-level of understanding of what goes on in a food label, let's list out a few basic parameters to look at while doing due diligence.

Serving Size and Calories

Nutrition Facts	
Serving Size 1/2 cup	
Servings Per Recipe 8	
Amount Per Serving	
Calories 190	Calories from Fat 80
	% Daily Value*
Total Fat 9g	12%
Saturated Fat 2.5g	13%
Trans Fat 0g	
Cholesterol 0mg	0%
Sodium 95mg	4%
Total Carbohydrate 24g	9%
Dietary Fiber 2g	7%
Sugars 9g	
Protein 5g	
Vitamin A 2% • Vitamin C 2%	
Calcium 4% • Iron 20%	
*Percent Daily Values are based on a 2,000 calorie diet. Your daily values may be higher or lower depending on your calorie needs.	

This is a trail mix, with eight servings in a container.[4,5] This means the total calorie count is not 190, but 190 × 8, that is, 1,520 calories. This package accounts almost entirely for Mihir's total daily calorie count, as we saw in the first chapter.

Now imagine if he consumes this entire trail mix under the false notion that it is 'healthy' because it has no sugar, no maida or no refined oil; he would overshoot his entire daily calorie count with this single trail mix packet. This would result in a 1,500+ calorie surplus as against his planned deficit of 165 calories.

'No Added Sugars', 'No Sugars' or 'Zero Carbs'

The uninformed consumer could take this claim at face value and assume this food to be healthy. But there are about ninety-seven chemicals that are labelled as sugars. If an ingredient ends in the letter 'ose', such as glucose or fructose, it is considered sugar.

Relative Sweetness of Sucrose and Other Sweet Substances[6]

Sweetener	Relative sweetness	Sweetener	Relative sweetness
fructose	1.2–1.8	saccharin	250–550
sucrose	1.00	aspartame	120–200
glucose	0.60	sucralose	550–750
maltose	~0.5	cyclamate	30–50
lactose	0.15–0.30	acesulfame K	~200
galactose	0.32	alitame	2000

[a]Refs. 12, 14–16.

If an ingredient ends in 'ol', such as maltitol or sorbitol, then also it is a sugar. However, it is not classified as sugar according to regulations, so manufacturers can use these ingredients and label them as 'no sugar'.

Here is a detailed list of sugars for your reference:

1. Agave
2. Barbados sugar
3. Barley malt
4. Barley malt syrup
5. Beet sugar
6. Blackstrap molasses
7. Brown rice syrup
8. Brown sugar
9. Buttercream
10. Buttered sugar
11. Cane juice
12. Cane sugar
13. Caramel
14. Carob syrup
15. Castor sugar
16. Chicory
17. Coconut palm sugar
18. Coconut sugar

19. Confectioners' sugar
20. Corn syrup
21. Corn syrup solids
22. Date paste
23. Date sugar
24. Dehydrated cane juice
25. Demerara sugar
26. Dextrin
27. Dextrose
28. Diastatic malt
29. Ethyl maltol
30. Evaporated cane juice
31. Florida crystals
32. Fructose
33. Fruit juice
34. Fruit juice concentrate
35. Galactose
36. Glucose
37. Glucose syrup solids
38. Golden sugar
39. Golden syrup
40. Granulated sugar
41. Grape sugar
42. High-fructose corn syrup
43. Honey
44. Icing sugar
45. Inositol
46. Invert sugar
47. Jaggery
48. Lactose
49. Malt syrup
50. Maltodextrin
51. Maltose
52. Mannose
53. Maple syrup
54. Molasses
55. Mono and diglycerides
56. Muscovado sugar
57. Natural sugars
58. Palm sugar
59. Panela sugar
60. Polycose
61. Polydextrin
62. Powdered sugar
63. Raw sugar
64. Rice syrup
65. Saccharose
66. Sorghum syrup
67. Sucanat
68. Sucrose
69. Sugar
70. Table sugar
71. Treacle
72. Xylose
73. Yellow sugar
74. Arabitol
75. Birch sugar
76. Erythritol
77. Glycerine
78. Glycerol
79. Hydrogenated starch hydrolysates
80. Isomalt

81. Lactitol
82. Maltitol
83. Mannitol
84. Sorbitol
85. Sugar alcohols
86. Xylitol
87. Ace-K
88. Acesulfame potassium
89. Advantame
90. Aspartame
91. Monk fruit sweetener
92. Neotame
93. Newtame
94. Saccharin
95. Splenda
96. Stevia
97. Sucralose

We know you didn't read all the names on this list; we just wanted to make a point.

You may also find high-fructose corn syrups in many of the foods as a replacement for sugar, but this is generally used because it tastes sweeter than sugar.[7] Sugars that form shorter and stronger hydrogen bonds with neighbouring water molecules taste sweeter.[8]

The first synthetic sweetener ever used was saccharin, discovered in 1878.[9] It is 300 times sweeter or, more accurately, 300 times more potent than sucrose, because it does not taste sweeter but can start to be tasted at lower concentrations. It was initially developed to compensate for sugar shortages during World War I but really took off in the 1960s when its taste was found to be improved by blending it with another artificial sweetener, cyclamate, discovered in 1937. From the 1960s onwards, chemists discovered other high-potency sweeteners, such as aspartame, sucralose and most recently neotame in 1992. Today, aspartame is the most widely used high-potency sweetener, and particularly when blended with other sweeteners, comes closest to reproducing the taste of sucrose.

Every other day, we may see a replacement for sugar, but it is just sugar coming to us in another avatar. Many ingredients aren't classified as sugars according to the regulations, so 'no added sugar' products with artificial sweeteners are sold to customers, who assume them to be 'healthy'.

The WHO had issued a stern warning against sweeteners in general, highlighting their questionable long-term effectiveness and health risks.[10]

But conflicting research from the Harvard Health Blogs also states, 'We simply do not have enough data to strongly recommend avoiding low-calorie sweeteners. We also don't have enough evidence to strongly endorse them. Until we have more research, it might be wise to decrease use of low-calorie sweeteners.'[11]

That last line is important—decrease use till we can be sure of efficacy.

A little bit of sugar is not going to kill you, but if you are a diabetic or someone with health issues, then being informed could be crucial to your long-term health. The more informed we are, the better we can guide someone else. Consumption of foods with these ingredients over the long run can have a detrimental impact on the body.

If you are reading this book fifty years down the line, just note that your sugar would have probably taken a new avatar.

'Net Carbs'

This is another term used to confuse consumers—net carbs are those that our body can fully absorb and hence derive calories from.

Net carbs = Total carbs minus fibre minus sugar alcohols

Fibres are carbs that the enzymes in our small intestine can't process. They pass through directly to our colon. Similarly, sugar-alcohols like maltitol, erythritol, etc., are only partially absorbed by the body. They do not enter the bloodstream in full. So, if you are on a low-carb diet, don't get fooled by this claim.

The real trouble with these claims is their psychological effect—most people who opt for foods with such low-carb claims are those trying to lose weight. Also remember that the most basic, inviolable equation for weight-loss is that 'calories in' must be less than 'calories out'.

If we eat more calories than we can burn, it doesn't matter which source they come from—whether the source is low-fat or no-carb or high-protein. The truth is that we will not lose weight in this way.

And that's where the 'net carb' claim hurts someone trying to lose weight. It's easy to pick up that 'zero-carb' bread and feel we haven't eaten much of anything at all. But remember that net carb, even if we believe the given definition, comes wrapped in fats and proteins, and hence, calories.

That is where a claim of 'net carbs' is going to hurt the individual running a caloric deficit. Be wary of all these terms.[12]

Ordering of Macronutrients

The FSSAI mandates the list of ingredients be in decreasing order of use. So, the most-used ingredient will be at the top.

A product that claims to be high in protein should have protein as the first ingredient in the list, especially since we'll buy the item for that purpose. But many items claiming to be 'high in protein' will actually have only 3–4 per cent of the calories coming from protein, which means these items are not what they claim.

Here are some thumb rules to follow according to the FSSAI:[13]
1. If a food has a daily value of 5 per cent or less for a nutrient, it is considered to be low in that nutrient.
2. A food is a good source of a nutrient if the daily value is between 10 per cent and 19 per cent.
3. If the daily value is 20 per cent or more, the food is considered an excellent source of that nutrient.

Nutritional Value

If there is an ingredient that has a number and no letter, it indicates that it has no nutritional value. The International Numbering System mandates that ingredients with no nutritional value should have a number. The European Union adds the letter E to classify such ingredients.[14]

Organic

If a food claims to be 'organic', it must contain 95 per cent of that organic ingredient.

The challenges for every individual reading this book would differ based on the infrastructure and regulations in their respective countries, but the principles of reading the label will largely remain the same. Luckily, there are now abundant tools available on the internet to empower us, just as we have tools to filter out stocks on the markets.

Let us use this ingredient due diligence screener hosted by Whole Truth Foods to do a quick search on three ingredients which are possibly the most consumed in our daily foods.[15]

Three of the most commonly used items in the household are bread, biscuits and butter. Our first preference would be to ditch the first two items on the list altogether, but since that is difficult for many people, let's see how we can filter out items.

Biscuits

Let's list the ingredients of a commonly available biscuit and ask the question—apart from salt, what do you recognize?

Wheat flour, sugar, vegetable oil (palm), glucose-fructose syrup, salt, raising agents (ammonium carbonates, sodium hydrogen bicarbonates), artificial flavours and emulsified (mono- and di-acetyl tartaric acid esters of mono- and di-glycerides of fatty acids).

Now let's pick out an ingredient to understand its implication—palm oil.

What Is Palm Oil?

Palm is made from the palm vegetable, also known as 'heart of palm'. It offers a greater yield at a lower cost of production as compared to any other vegetable oils.

Why Is It Bad?

It has high amounts of saturated fats, and refined palm oil could contain carcinogens (substances capable of causing cancer in living tissue).

What Should I Do?

Avoid.

Bread

Let's list the ingredients of a commonly available loaf of bread and ask the question—apart from salt, what do you recognize?

Refined wheat flour, yeast, sugar, virtual gluten, iodized salt, preservative, improvers, acidity regulator, vitamins.

What Is Acidity Regulator INS 260, or Acetic Acid?

Acetic acid is produced from vinegar, or is synthetically produced from wood fibre or methanol. It's used to control the acidic or alkaline nature of packaged foods.

Why Is It Bad?

Consumption by some individuals or in large quantities can cause vomiting, nausea and diarrhoea. Over-consumption can result in tooth decay.

What Should I Do?

It's okay to consume in moderation.

Butter

Butter may contain what is called margarine at the back of the label.

What Is Margarine?

Margarine is used as a substitute for butter in flavouring, baking and cooking. Most margarine consumed today is made from vegetable oil.

Why Is It Bad?

It contains trans fats that can raise people's LDL cholesterol and can also reduce levels of HDL cholesterol.

These effects can raise the risk of heart attacks, strokes and type-2 diabetes.

What Should I Do?
Avoid.

In situations like these, ask yourself two simple questions to make life easier:
1. Do I know what this ingredient is? If not, then why should I consume it?
2. Can I find a safer alternative after going through the first step?

To make this process concise—if we don't have the patience to go through the entire ingredient list, it is better to go through at least the nutrition facts. So, let's say we just can't give up that loaf of bread. Then, we should go for the loaf of bread that has the higher amount of fibre compared to total carbohydrates. At least fibre would keep us full. We can start with these small changes and then progress slowly.

If we start too fast, we will get overwhelmed.

ThePrint broke down a survey conducted by the Indian Council of Medical Research's National Institute of Nutrition (ICMR-NIN).[16]

INDIANS' LABEL READING HABIT ON PACKAGED FOOD IS MOSTLY LIMITED TO EXPIRY DATE

% of respondents who do not read these items on the labels of packaged food items when buying

Item	Don't read	Always read
Expiry date	13	74
Brand name	23	61
Manufacturing date	25	58
Ingredients	58	15
Veg and Non veg symbol	61	20
Storage	63	14
Nutrient Information	63	9
Allergen	72	8

Note: Based on a survey of 3231 respondents aged 18-60, conducted in Delhi, Pune, Hyderabad, Kolkata and Jorhat. Nutrition information's statistic is based on the average of 9 nutrients.
Source: National Institute of Nutrition

Source: *ThePrint*

The survey highlights the clear lack of cognizance of the consumer in India in terms of looking out for the most important part of a nutrition label—only 9 per cent of consumers read the nutrient information and only 15 per cent read the ingredients list. The brand name and expiry date are the most important information for the consumer.

Studies have shown how changing of attitudes towards nutrition greatly benefitted students at an early age. A study in the journal *Neurotherapeutics* showed how additives in food could have been linked to ADHD in students.[17]

An interesting case study came from Chile, which implemented the Law of Food Labelling and Advertising in 2016, comprising of mandatory front-of-package (FOP) warning labels, restrictions on child-directed marketing, and the banning of sales in schools of all foods and beverages containing added sugars, sodium or saturated fats that exceeded set nutrient or calorie thresholds.[18] The FOP labels displayed a black stop sign that used warning words of 'high in' followed by sugar, sodium, saturated fat or calories. Later analyses found that purchases of sweetened beverages significantly declined following the implementation of this multifaceted law, which was more effective than prior single initiatives, such as a tax on sweetened beverages.

Another study, conducted in 2017 by the United States' National Bureau of Economic Research, found that when a school signed a contract with a healthy lunch company, students began scoring better on end-of-year academic tests.[19] On average, student test scores were 0.03 to 0.04 standard deviations higher (about four percentile points). Not only that, the test score increases were about 40 per cent larger for students who qualified for reduced-price or free school lunches—these students were the most likely to eat the school lunches.

In India, the FSSAI has started to take positive actions to improve the nutrition and health standards for outlets. According to their new regulations, 'restaurants having central licences or outlets at ten or more locations will need to display the "calorific value in kcal per serving and serving size" of food items on menu cards, booklets or boards'.[20]

In fact, a study conducted by *The BMJ* in 2018 in the United States showed that calorie labels in fast-food outlets lead to a small drop in calories purchased.[21]

Applying the Same Practices to Investing

In the same way that a consumer buys packaged food without doing basic due diligence on the contents, they could also invest into a stock without doing basic due diligence on the financial statements.

This is a blueprint to determine whether a stock is actually worth our time or not. It becomes a lot easier to avoid mishaps when we have a certain set of principles in place.

1. Invest in what you understand.
2. Do not judge a book by its cover.

Let us take the hypothetical examples of four companies—Company A grew its revenue by 30 per cent year on year. Company B grew its revenue by 35 per cent year on year. Company C will be raising Rs 10,000 crore to pay off its debt. Company D has won an order worth Rs 5,000 crore, so the future is bright.

Are all these companies doing well?

An investor who has not spent enough time in the financial markets would think this information is enough to invest in these companies.

Ankush often get calls from clients at work, and they tell him he should be looking at these companies to invest their money, based on these single pieces of information.

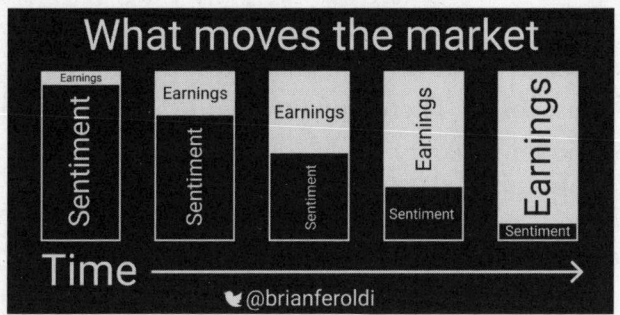

Source: Brian Feroldi

This graphic by Brian Feroldi encapsulates what moves stock prices. In the short run, it is, in fact, sentiment, which is affected by news, rumours, and even whims and fancies. In the longer run, sentiment does matter, but in a very small way. The earnings of the company become far more important—not only the quantity of earnings, but also the quality and sustainability.

Take a look at this stock: the company's revenue is growing at a breakneck pace and the price is rising in the short term on the 'revenue' figures. Most investors rush in at this time with this little piece of information.

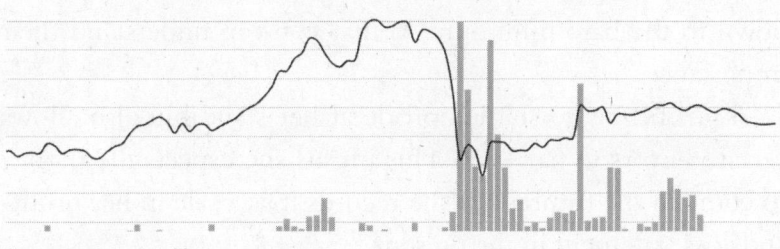

Source: screener.in

Had an investor rushed in at this juncture based on this single piece of information, she would have got sucked into the euphoria of the peak of the stock price, and gone on to make a loss of close to 60 per cent for over three years.

The reason would be that the investor simply judged the book by its cover. There are three critical elements that an investor should look at:
1. Profit-and-loss statement
2. Cash-flow statement
3. Balance sheet

Most investors are either lazy or merely confirm their positive biases with limited data. They fail to navigate beyond the news flashes, social media tips and the barrage of information that gets thrown at them from all sides. Even those who do make an attempt at looking at financial statements often do not navigate through the finer details. The balance sheet is also a crucial element, and, in fact, arguably the *most important*. One could even say it is prudent to first look at the health of the balance sheet before even moving to the P&L and cash-flow statement.

Changes in key elements of the business in the balance sheet over the years reflect on the cash-flow statement.

However, the layman may not understand these two statements apart from the P&L so we will simplify it down to the bare minimum so that you can understand their importance.

A girl begins to sell lemonade at her stand but also allows certain buyers to pay later. This means she expects the money to come in the future, but she records it as a sale in her profit-and-loss statement in the present.

Now, let's take a look at her finances:

Particulars (Rs)	Year 1	Year 2
Sales (A)	100	140
Cost of Goods Sold (B)	20	28
Gross Profit (C) = (A) - (B)	80	112
Other Expenses (D)	5	10
Depreciation (E)	10	14
Finance Costs (F)	15	17
Particulars (Rs)	**Year 1**	**Year 2**
Profit Before Tax (G)= (C) - (D) - (E) - (F)	50	71
Tax (H)	15	20
Profit After Tax (I) = (G) - (H)	35	51

Explaining these key line items:
- *Sales:* The entry she records as a sale to her customer.
- *Cost of Goods Sold:* The cost of buying lemons from the local market, salt, and other daily ingredients she may require to make the lemonade. This expense pertains only to the cost of ingredients related to sale of that year. All unsold ingredients are carried over as inventory in the balance sheet.
- *Depreciation:* The implicit cost of the wear and tear of the table she bought for the stand, the jugs she uses to keep the lemonade, and other such assets that gradually lose value over time. These will need to be replaced over some years.
- *Finance Cost:* The interest she has agreed to pay her parents each month for the money she borrowed from them.
- *Tax:* Amount she has to pay to the government based on the excellent profits she is reporting.

The girl has managed to grow the profitability of her company 'on paper', a good sign for the layman at face value. If this were a listed business, you would have certainly seen news flashes like '40 per cent YoY growth in revenues', 'Lemonade stand run by a dynamic young entrepreneur has just posted a solid set of numbers, growing the bottom line by 45 per cent', 'High growth, high margin business—this girl is achieving the impossible'.

Let's observe her basic balance sheet to understand how she finances her business, what assets she owns, who owe her money from her business and who she owes money. This is her balance sheet at the end of Year 1.

Liabilities	Rs	Assets	Rs
Equity	0	Inventory	50
Add: Profits	35	Debtors	80
Loans	200	Fixed assets	90
Accrued interest	15	Cash on hand	30
Total	*250*	*Total*	*250*

Explaining these key line items:
Liabilities: The sources of her funds
- *Equity:* The money put in by herself, which is zero in this case.
- *Long-Term Borrowings:* The loan she has taken from her parents to kick off her business.
- *Accrued Interest:* She did not actually pay the interest on the loan taken from her parents but accrued it, which means that she had added the amount to the loan outstanding.
- *Payables:* The money she owes her regular suppliers of lemonade, salt, sugar and other items she needs for supply of her business. She did not get any credit and hence had to pay in cash. This translates to nil creditors.

Assets: The usage of her funds
- *Inventory:* The lemonade, sugar, salt and other items she needs to use to make her lemonade. It can't sit unused for too long else it will become rotten.
- *Receivables:* The money she has to receive from customers—her friends and family, who promise to pay her later for the glasses of lemonade she gave them without taking cash upfront.
- *Fixed Assets:* The tables, chairs, banners and other items she needs to invest in for her lemonade stand.
- *Cash in Hand:* After accounting for all these items, this is the amount of cash left in her hand from her parents' loan. It will keep depleting year on year for these expenses and eventually when it drops to zero, she has to makes sure she is making enough cash from her business so that she doesn't have to go back to her parents for another loan.

This is how her balance sheet looks in Year 2.

Liabilities	Rs	Assets	Rs
Equity	35	Inventory	60
Add: Profits	51	Debtors	180
Loans	200	Fixed assets	76
Interest payable on loans	32	Cash on hand	2
Total	*318*	*Total*	*318*

Now that we know her P&L on paper and how she funds her business, let's move to whether her business is actually making money or not:

Particulars	Year 1	Year 2
PAT	35	51
Add: Depreciation	10	14
Cash from operations before WC changes	45	65
Cash used/released from Debtors	-80	-100
Cash used/released from Inventory	-50	-10
Cash used/released from Creditors	0	0
Cash from Operations	*-85*	*-45*
Particulars	**Year 1**	**Year 2**
Loans taken/repaid	200	0
Interest accrued but not paid	15	17
Cash from financing activities	*215*	*17*
Fixed Assets purchased	-100	0
Cash from investing activities	*-100*	*0*
Net Cash Movement	30	-28
Opening Cash	0	30
Closing Cash	*30*	*2*

We see a different picture with the cash-flow statement, the girl is actually making a *loss*.

Receivables, payables and inventory are balance sheet items, however, changes in their values over a year can reflect changes in cash flow coming or going out.

Don't Judge a Book by Its Cover

Let's delve deeper into the girl's cash-flow statement by using our basic level understanding of her P&L and balance sheet.

The cash-flow statement will give us an idea of how much cash this girl is actually making.

Depreciation: The cost that was covered in the P&L however, this is not a real cost as the money is not going out of our hands, it is just the loss in value of the tables, chairs and stand over time. So we add this back to the profit to arrive at the cash profit or cash from operations before working capital changes.

Changes in Receivables: The people who owe her money are not picking up the phone and some have even gone missing, leading to a case of lesser revenue being realized in cash as compared with revenue actually reported.

At the end of Year 1 her receivables have increased by Rs 80 which means that she has to collect Rs 80 more, hence much less cash is available to her. This is a negative for her cash balance hence we deduct it in the cash-flow statement.

At the end of Year 2 her receivables have increased to Rs 180. She is owed Rs 100 more than what she was owed the previous year which is again a negative for her cash balance hence we deduct it in the cash-flow statement.

Changes in Inventory: The value of the unsold inventory has gone up as the girl was not able to sell as much of the raw materials that she bought.

She is unable to sell it, continues to buy more of the items to make her lemonade but is unable to sell that equivalent amount.

She is putting cash into the business without being able to make more money out of it.

If one were to analyse deeper, one may even say 'Hey, year-old lemons are of no use. The inventories are clearly not worth

Rs 60 in Year 2 but they are being artificially shown on the balance sheet.'

Changes in Payables: There is no relief here. Because vendors are wary of the business skills of this girl, they require her to put up cash in order to buy material. The girl is getting a taste of the real world here.

Finance Cost: This is the actual interest expense she has to pay to her parents for the loan. Since it's a loan from her parents, she has convinced them to not take the interest payment in cash but merely account for it, as we saw with the accrued interest line item on the balance sheet. Hence, it's added back to her cash-flow statement.

Tax Expenses: This is the actual cash expense that she paid to the authorities on the reported profit, hence it is already deducted from the profits and not adjusted in the cashflow statement.

Fixed Assets Purchased: These are the equipment she has purchased to run her stand. Starting out with Rs 100 worth of equipment, the same have been depreciated every year.

Our poor little girl is actually running a *cash loss* in both Year 1 and Year 2 despite seeing excellent growth in her revenue and profitability.

She had been allowing a set of customers to pay her after a while and is now having a difficult time recovering the money from them but she had recorded this transaction as a sale hence creating an illusion for someone who never moved past the profit-and-loss statement.

She has two options now:
- Ask her parents to give her money to continue running the store

- Shut down or sell the business to avoid further losses

What we learnt here is that the girl was simply earning a paper profit and not actually getting the cash in her hands.

Fortunately for her, most investors simply look at the profit-and-loss statement, and they would probably invest in her business without even glancing at the cash-flow statement.

As a result, she would likely get an investment from an investor almost every single time.

An investor simply taking profits at face value for the *short term* would eventually succumb to the pain of the company not being able to make enough cash in the *long term*.

Even media articles will focus mainly on the headline numbers of profit and loss, which pique investor interests. Cash flow makes for a boring article—most people won't even be aware of what cash flows are, so it is pointless to report on that.

However, the value of a business in the stock market is a derivative of its long-term cash flows discounted to the present.

As easy as this concept sounds, you will be surprised to know how few investors adhere to this basic principle.

Now, let's make it slightly more complicated with another hypothetical example. But while we go through this, let's try to keep in mind the lessons from the girl selling lemonade.

Let's say this hypothetical company is called Frontline Numbers Company, and assume it is a well-established healthcare company based in India, engaged in the development and manufacturing of various products.

Scenario: Over the past few years, Frontline Numbers Company has been investing heavily in research and development to create new, innovative drugs and expand its product portfolio. As a result of these investments, the company has seen a significant increase in its reported profits due to accounting principles related to revenue recognition and amortization of R&D expenses over time.

Explanation: The company's profits grew rapidly due to accounting practices, such as recognizing revenue from sales of new drugs and amortizing the R&D expenses over several years. As per accounting standards, these practices allow the company to show profits on its income statement but the cash flows may be pointing to a completely different picture.

If you are a lay reader unfamiliar with accounting, did you understand a single word of this?

Regardless of whether you knew this company was tweaking its profit numbers or not, had you gone to the cash-flow statement, chances are you would not have been enamoured by the profitability numbers, because you cannot make these adjustments in the cash-flow statement.

In reality, the company may be facing challenges in converting its reported profits into actual cash.[22]

This situation can arise because of various factors, such as extended credit terms offered to customers, slow collections from customers, high inventory levels, or substantial investments in fixed assets. It is not the fault of the company; it is the fault of the investor who is not digging deeper to get more answers.

Just like how it was not the fault of the food manufacturer that the consumer was not willing to dig deeper into the food label.

This is what the stock performance chart of the Frontline Numbers Company would look like from 2019 to 2022.

Don't Judge a Book by Its Cover

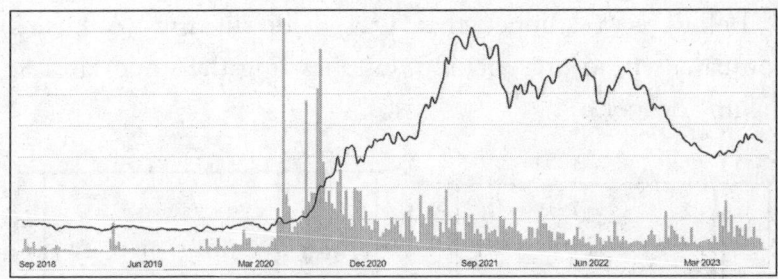

Source: screener.in

Now, do not get us wrong—it is proven that the long-term stock price performance converges with the earnings growth of the company. But the profit only means something if it's going to get converted into real cash. Just like calories in food only mean something if they are contributing to our long-term health.

The chart shows an upward trend in the stock price, indicating that investors initially responded positively to the reported profit growth and optimistic prospects of the company due to its accounting practices. The steep increase in the stock price from 2020 to 2021 corresponds to the period when Frontline Numbers Company was reporting significant profit growth due to revenue recognition and R&D expense amortization.

The company had also announced the planned launch of a new drug, news that investors took to very keenly.

However, towards the latter part of 2021 and extending into 2022, investors and the market would start to realize that the reported profits have not translated into equivalent cash-flow growth, and may not do so anytime soon. This realization would lead to an almost 60 per cent fall in the stock price.

You would have lost almost all your money in these companies in the highlighted pictures below too back in 2008 observing this same phenomenon if you judged a book by its cover.

Below is a snippet that was made in my (Ankush's) company's fund presentation, emphasizing the importance of digging deeper.

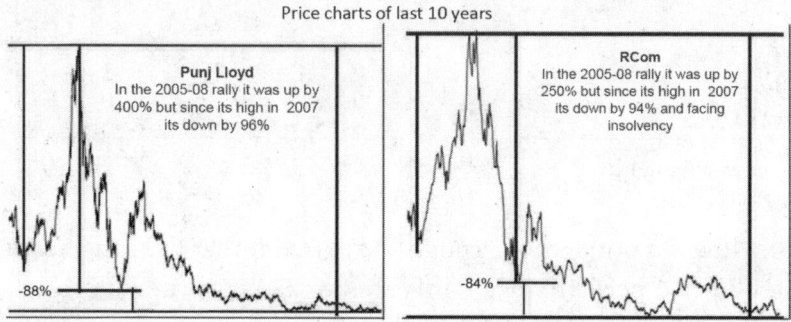

Source: Bloomberg and PhillipCapital[23]

Most individuals pursue 'multibagger stocks' in the hope of quick returns, just as they consume junk food without conducting due diligence. The detrimental effects of judging a book by its cover become apparent later, as we will discover in our chapter on delayed gratification.

Now, let's examine another fictional company, which we'll call the Boring Slow Grower. This company typically stays out of the sensational headlines and maintains consistent growth. It may not be captivating enough to attract attention or spark investor interest. In fact, such companies are rarely found in individual investor portfolios, and even if they are included, they typically constitute a minimal portion of the overall portfolio because of their lack of glamour.

Observe the Boring Slow Grower's chart over a short term of three years—there's barely any movement, and even flat performance, despite posting strong fundamental numbers of cash-flow growth.

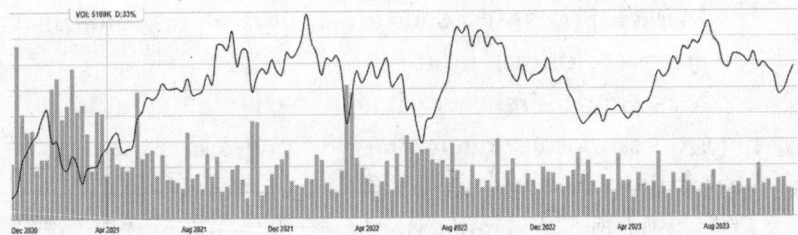

Source: screener.in

However, now, zoom out and see the performance for the last ten years for Boring Slow Grower.

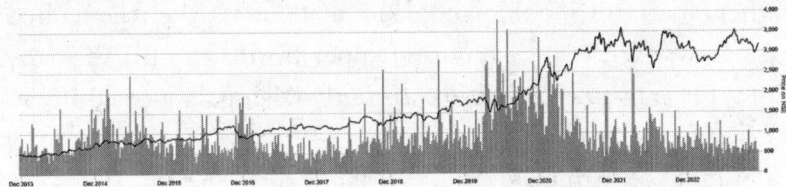

Source: screener.in

In these ten years, an investment of Rs 100 into Boring Slow Grower would have become Rs 1,000.

You may ask, if one does not understand the health of the company's financials, why would one invest hard-earned money in it? The answer is that frontline numbers can create an optical illusion for the investor.

The late American investor John Bogle rightly pointed out, 'Sooner or later, the rewards of investing must be based on future cash flows. The purpose of any stock market, after all, is to simply provide liquidity for stock in return for the promise of future cash flows, enabling investors to realize the present value of a future stream of income at any time.'

Research demonstrates that markets determine the prices of stocks, just like any other financial asset, in two ways:

1. Market prices respond to changes in a company's prospects for cash flow.
2. Market prices reflect cash flows well into the future.

Investors cannot accurately conclude long-term valuations of an asset without having some idea of the company's cash flows.

The profit-and-loss and cash-flow statements of fraudulent companies can paint very different pictures. A large number of companies have also been found cooking their books and have seen significant erosion in their stock prices subsequently.

One of the common traits of the companies mentioned earlier (apart from cooking books) is that none of them generated cash flows. While they reported super-normal profits in many cases, these businesses were constantly raising debt or equity to survive.

Some companies even reported positive cash flows by falsifying cash balances in financial statements.

This is a step even beyond the fancies of an experienced investor, and many investors often unknowingly burn their hands in these companies.

Key Principles Learned from This Chapter

- Don't just judge the nutritional aspect of a packaged item by its cover; dig deeper beyond the calorie and macronutrient count.
- On the investing front, don't judge a company purely by its revenue and profitability; dig deeper into the cash-flow statement.
- We should avoid buying a food whose nutritional value we do not understand, or the stock of a company whose financial metrics we do not understand.

- The front of any nutrition package or financial statement is mostly marketing; as we dig deeper, we can verify the claim for ourselves.
- The shorter the list of ingredients, the higher the probability of better safety (though not always). The simpler the financials of a company, the higher the probability of the company not fudging numbers.
- Financial statements and nutritional labels can be strategically drawn up to show that the end product is harmless. These practices are not illegal; it is upon the cognizance of the investor and consumer to be aware.

7

The Pain and Value of Paying

There is no such thing as free advice. Free is a price you pay. Let these words sink in.

The one question that most individuals are not able to get past comfortably when trying to take up any service that could possibly add value to their lives is 'how much does it cost'. This is especially true when talking about health or investing services. This phenomenon is known as the pain of paying, and there is a psychological and neurological reason for it.

The concept was explained by Dan Ariely and Jeff Kreisler in their book *Dollars and Sense*, and a large part of this chapter is inspired by the psychology they laid out.[1]

The phenomenon states that the more time we spend mentally accounting for how the money we've spent will generate value, the more pain we feel.[2]

Decisions such as hiring a financial coach or a health coach fit into this category, as per our experience. On the other hand, spending money on our favourite greasy snacks while lounging on our couch has the opposite effect—it's a painless feeling.

The more we contemplate our spending, the more painful it becomes. If we happen to consume or experience something while thinking about the payment, the pain of paying worsens, making the experience seem far less valuable than it actually is.

The book gives the example of a great holiday—when we pay for our expenses upfront and can simply enjoy the experience, we appreciate that cocktail more, savour that dinner more, and have a better time with water sports. However, when we have to pay a large sum after experiencing these activities on the holiday, a part of the fun psychologically diminishes. We don't make the rules; this is just how our brains work.

Neuroimaging and MRI scans have shown that paying does indeed stimulate the same regions of the brain involved in physical pain. And when we experience pain, our first instinct is to avoid it. However, what occurs in this process is that we often transition from painful spending to painless spending.

Painless spending includes indulging in multiple nights out, regularly spending money on junk food, and engaging in many painless activities like buying a stock and selling it after making 20 per cent gains, and hoping we can do it again and again.

Remember what we explained about cheap dopamine? These painless spending activities release just that. Paying for something that doesn't require effort or commitment doesn't hurt as much, and we humans prefer easy and painless options.

Avoiding a certain level of pain causes us to lose our focus on the actual value we receive in exchange for the pain of paying. This, in turn, leads to a phenomenon called 'borrowed conviction', a term in market lingo for free advice taken from an individual without having paid for their services, stemming from our inability or reluctance to pay for an adviser to guide us in important decisions.

This explains why we tend to place trust in someone else's free advice without investing the time to conduct our own research—it's a process that is both painless and easy.

This plays out spectacularly in the stock markets in the lure of quick and easy money.

Trading in futures and options in the financial markets is, in fact, one of the most dangerous ways of playing with our money. If we really want to participate, we ought to hand over the management of the money full-time to a trusted organization or professional, but the probability of making money is still low regardless.

An influencer giving you free unsolicited advice on social media also comes under this category.

If you have watched the streaming show *Scam 1992*, there is a story arc where a young individual with no experience in the stock market makes a good amount of money on futures and options taking tips from Harshad Mehta. He makes money while the going is good, but loses everything and eventually dies by suicide when the markets crash.

In fact, a SEBI study even showed how nine out of ten traders lose money while trading in derivatives.[3] Despite knowing this, retail traders keep coming back for more.

An October 2023 study by Axis Mutual, titled 'Gamification of Indian Equities', highlights a stark truth—that with options now available for day-trading of futures, the volumes of futures and options have gone up.[4] This typically takes place when the market is doing well, but ends badly when the market eventually comes down.

The study highlights another interesting data point. 'In fantasy sports, the take rate of the pot is 15 per cent. For every hundred put in by the retail participants, they get eighty-five back. The skew is the opposite in derivatives, with only

The Pain and Value of Paying

15 per cent of the pot coming back to retail. As per a recent SEBI study in FY22, retail traders on aggregate lost more than 80 per cent of their bets (Rs 45,000 crore was lost by 90 per cent of participants while 10 per cent of the participants earned Rs 6,900 crore),' it states.

Despite all these warnings, even today, investors continue to make the same mistakes in the markets in the lure of quick money, with free unsolicited advice.

A sound financial adviser helps you not only with their expertise in the subject but also ensures you do not make behavioural mistakes. You are not just paying for the financial advice—financial advice, after a point of time, is essentially the same 3-4 boring maxims repeated over and over again. A sound financial adviser ensures you stick on the path.

In the same way, a sound fitness trainer ensures you stay the path. The exercises and eating plans are a small part of the advice.

In fact, this is an interesting note on the importance of hand-holding through an adviser.[5]

Table 1: How SIP data is being interpreted...		
SIP accounts with tenure	Total SIP accounts (June 2023)	% SIP accounts
> 5years	80,76,235	12%
> 4 yrs upto 5 yrs	48,69,096	7%
> 3 yrs upto 4 yrs	45,20,552	7%
> 2 yrs upto 3 yrs	80,23,063	12%
> 1 yr upto 2 yrs	1,57,09,198	24%
Less than 1 yr	2,53,38,889	38%
Total	6,65,37,033	100%
Interpretation: Oh gosh! Only 12% of SIPs have tenure of over 5 years! Investors don't continue their SIPs for long enough.. Maybe they lose trust in SIPs after some time...		

Table 2: How SIP data needs to be interpreted...			
Number of SIP accounts outstanding		Tenure wise number of SIP accounts as of June 2023	% active as of June 2023
5 years back (June 2018)	2,29,00,000	> 5 years — 80,76,235	35%
4 years back (June 2019)	2,73,00,000	> 4 years — 1,29,45,331	47%
3 years back (June 2020)	3,23,00,000	> 3 years — 1,74,65,883	54%
2 years back (June 2021)	4,02,00,000	> 2 years — 2,54,88,946	63%
1 year back (June 2022)	5,54,00,000	> 1 year — 4,11,98,144	74%
Interpretation: 35% of the SIP accounts have continued for over 5 years, 47% for over 4 years and 54% for over 3 years... And yes, discontinuation of SIP from a mutual fund scheme doesn't mean an investor has lost trust in SIPs... they may have started a SIP in other scheme(s)			
Data source: AMFI, news publications.			

Source: Nilesh Naik, LinkedIn

The data here suggests that only 12 per cent of all SIP investors maintain an investment horizon of more than five years. The percentage of investors who stick around decreases as the years pass, even though the irony is that the bulk of wealth accumulation typically begins after the fifth year. Yes, there may be instances where investors shift their SIP to another fund due to the underperformance of the current fund, but based on my (Ankush's) experience interacting with investors, many tend to discontinue the SIP altogether.

Traditionally, investors tend to exit the market when negative news about market conditions spreads.

In my (Ankush's) professional experience, I recall many such incidents from 2020, when investors were panicking due to the market crash caused by Covid-19. Many investors had been enjoying healthy returns since 2016, but one unprecedented year erased the memory of preceding years, which is typically how the psychology of most investors plays out.

I personally advised a few of my friends and family, who were managing their own investments to ignore the noise and stay focussed on their long-term goals and investment process.

Fidelity Investments conducted a study on which investor portfolios performed the best during this time, and their finding was, 'those who were dead' or 'those who had forgotten that they have an account.'[6] This implies that those who invested for long periods of time by forgetting their portfolios were those who did best.

Data from Edelweiss Asset Management in 2023 highlights some interesting data.[7] A breakdown of the money invested in mutual funds by individual investors reveals that over 77 per cent of their investments are made through regular plans.

Furthermore, when we examine the holding period data for equity and hybrid schemes, we find that 32 per cent of investors remain invested in the scheme for over twenty-four months when using a regular plan, compared to just 14 per cent when investing through a direct plan.

A regular plan is one in which an investor invests through an adviser, while a direct plan is where they invest on their own. A regular plan comes with a fee for the advice and hand-holding the adviser provides.

A similar narrative unfolds in the health and fitness space. In fact, managing our health and nutrition without guidance can be even more perilous than managing our finances without knowledge, as each person's body is unique and health is more fragile than money.

Ankush's Story

In 2014, I lost a significant amount of weight while preparing for a marathon, especially muscle mass, which is common among marathon runners. To regain muscle, I consulted a highly regarded nutritionist, who explained that achieving a 'calorie surplus' and consuming more calories than needed is a gradual process. However, I expressed my desire to accomplish this within three months. While I did gain weight, it was mostly excess fat.

Starting that year, I began to educate myself about calorie management for maintaining, losing or gaining weight. It took nearly three years of consistent effort to achieve the desired weight gain.

After three years, I approached the nutritionist again, acknowledging that she had been right, and gained an understanding of her emphasis on the importance of setting realistic expectations and recognizing that the process can be slow and uneventful. Having a grasp of calorie management has greatly benefited in various aspects of my life.

Managing expectations is often what a good adviser does, and we often fall prey to wanting fast outcomes, which happened to me. But now, I have control over my weight, regardless of my exercise regimen or busy work schedule.

The nutritionist's ultimate goal was to empower me to manage meals independently. She never made unrealistic promises, such as achieving a ripped or jacked physique in three months, as some unsolicited advice from social media influencers might lead one to believe.

By treating the cost of hiring a nutritionist as capital expenditure, we can be seen to be investing in improving the quality of our most important asset—health.

I had similar experiences with multiple personal trainers—I would hire one for six months, not see any results, and time and again, assume that it was the trainer's poor coaching techniques. While the trainer knew that the process of achieving the goal of building muscles would take years of coming to the gym and working out consistently, doing the same old things incrementally better, it would not be in the interests of the gym for him to communicate that to me and probably lose a client.

Most trainers are forced to create fancy custom plans to retain them, else the client would feel a loss of novelty. This is one of the key reasons why individuals fail to stick with a personal trainer for long, and most trainers I speak to give similar feedback.

Ten years down the line, after I did learn on my own, I went back to that first trainer to tell him he was right. This book would probably have been a pipe dream had I not paid for the lessons I learnt back then from the trainer and nutritionist.

An academic study on how personal one-on-one training improves gym performance found that 57 per cent of the subjects showed upward movement.[8] Furthermore, if those who could not move up a stage (because they were in the highest stage) were factored out, then an even more impressive 73 per cent of the clients showed upward stage movement after the ten-week intervention. While this was a study with a small control group and a very short timeframe, it does provide an idea as to how working with a fitness coach improves the probability of success.

Working with professionals removes these issues, because we pass on accountability. Paying them leads to that sense of accountability.

A trainer and nutritionist are accountable for ensuring we stick to the plan that we have given them, if they are to receive future referrals for their business or continue building a relationship with us.

We strive to 'save money' and avoid 'wasting money', even though trusted experts can, for a fee, explain how to save even more and waste even less of that money.

Even though we have limited knowledge of how our bodies work, we attempt to adopt nutritional habits found on the internet without seeking advice from experts, simply because of the associated costs. Experts in these fields are individuals who have dedicated countless years to honing their skills in order to provide value to us. When we pay them, we're not compensating them solely for an hour of consultation or for a certificate/degree they earned; we are paying them for their years of cumulative experience.

While we have discussed the cost of professionals, genuine relationships with advisers are constructed not only based on cost and value but also on the strength of the relationship itself. Individuals entrust their most valuable assets, their health and wealth, to our guidance, often considering the prospective relationship they can develop with us. Hiring an adviser entails more than just an economic expense.

The assessment of the value of employing a professional should also encompass opportunity costs, which refer to the implicit costs incurred by avoiding the expenditure on a professional's services.

This phenomenon can be frequently observed in the financial sector, where an investor's reluctance to pay an additional fee can, more often than not, result in higher long-term costs in terms of their returns.

Many individuals will blindly invest in the wrong asset classes, consume inappropriate foods, and engage in improper exercise routines, solely to avoid an expense, often without recognizing the substantial opportunity costs they are actually incurring.

Frequently, those lacking expertise in either field end up bearing a significant opportunity cost, which is challenging for an individual to quantify.

Key Principles Learned from This Chapter

- If we are focussing on value addition by hiring a personal financial coach or health coach, we must be cognizant of the value we derive over the longer term, and ask ourselves if we can consistently generate that value on our own. If we cannot, it is better to seek an adviser.
- If value exceeds cost, the money is well-spent.
- The pain of paying is what keeps us from most valuable activities in life.

8

Twisting the Data

American author Dan Heath wrote, 'Data are just summaries of thousands of stories—tell a few of those stories to help make the data meaningful.'[1] Let us illustrate what he means. Ask yourself, value or growth, which strategy works best in investing?

Low carb or keto, which strategy works best in nutrition? If we assemble our data correctly, we can convince you of anything, because we can always find research to demonstrate that each style of nutrition or investing works better than the other.

There is a term called 'survivorship bias'—a tendency to focus on the individuals or things that have survived or succeeded, while ignoring those that did not. It can lead to skewed conclusions or strategies based on incomplete data, as the failures or 'non-survivors' are often overlooked.

Humans are psychologically enamoured by survivors when, in actuality, they should study the non-survivors to see what should not have been done.

There is absolutely no problem in backing our claims with data; in fact, it is the only ethical way to present facts. However, the problem is that individuals use data from one strategy to criticize another strategy, as we often see on Twitter (now X) among affluent individuals in the investing and health space.

Easy access to information hasn't necessarily made our lives easier, but actually tougher. There are thousands of diet books available on Amazon, so naturally, not all of them can be correct. There are a hundred types of diets, and similarly, hundreds of ways to invest, yet not all of them can be right. But we will be bombarded with information constantly.

Let's begin with the various types of diets, and see how each one has its merits and drawbacks.

Our understanding of whether a specific nutrition plan is effective or not primarily comes from two types of studies: epidemiology and clinical trials.

According to Dr Peter Attia's book *Outlive*, epidemiological studies are observational in nature and aim to understand disease patterns and potential risk factors in populations.[2] Clinical trials, on the other hand, are experimental studies that focus on evaluating the safety and effectiveness of medical interventions—such as drugs, vaccines, medical devices or behavioural therapies—in human subjects. While epidemiological studies observe naturally occurring events, clinical trials involve intentional interventions in controlled conditions.

Although these studies provide direction about the efficacy of a diet, it is not certain whether they would work for every individual or not. There are a lot of subjective factors involved, so one should understand how their own diet is affecting their health rather than taking studies at simply face value.

Let us show you how data can be cherry picked by defining a diet and backing claims with studies to 'prove' its efficacy.

Ketogenic Diet

This is a high-fat, low-carbohydrate diet that has been studied for various health benefits. Here are two studies that demonstrate some of its advantages:

Study 1: 'The effects of a ketogenic diet on exercise metabolism and physical performance in off-road cyclists'[3]

The researchers found that athletes following a ketogenic diet experienced significantly higher fat oxidation rates during exercise, indicating that the body was utilizing fat for energy more efficiently. This suggests that the ketogenic diet might enhance the body's ability to use fat as a fuel source during exercise, potentially improving endurance in athletes.

Study 2: 'A ketogenic diet favourably affects serum biomarkers for cardiovascular disease in normal-weight men'[4]

This study found that the ketogenic diet led to significant improvements in various cardiovascular risk factors, including decreased levels of triglycerides, LDL (bad) cholesterol and blood glucose. At the same time, HDL (good) cholesterol levels increased. These changes suggest that a ketogenic diet might have a positive impact on cardiovascular health by improving lipid profiles and reducing risk factors associated with heart disease.

Carnivore Diet

This is a dietary regimen that involves consuming only animal products and excludes all plant-based foods. The carnivore diet has shown effectiveness in promoting weight loss, improving mental clarity and reducing inflammation in certain individuals.

Study 1: 'Effectiveness and safety of a novel care model for the management of type 2 diabetes at one year: an open-label, non-randomized, controlled study'[5]

Participants showed significant improvements in glycaemic control, weight loss and reduction in diabetes-related medications following this dietary approach.

Study 2: 'Clinical experience of a diet designed to reduce ageing'[6, 7]

The report suggested that participants experienced weight loss, improved blood lipid profiles and better overall health markers while adhering to the animal-based dietary regimen.

Paleo Diet

Also known as the Palaeolithic or 'caveman diet', this involves consuming whole foods similar to those available to our ancient ancestors, focussing on lean meats, fish, fruits, vegetables, nuts and seeds while excluding processed foods, grains, legumes and dairy products.

Study 1: 'Metabolic and physiological improvements from consuming a palaeolithic, hunter-gatherer type diet'[8]

Participants following the Palaeo diet experienced significant improvements in glucose tolerance, blood pressure, body weight and other cardiovascular risk factors compared to the control group following a traditional diabetes diet.

Study 2: 'A palaeolithic diet confers higher insulin sensitivity, lower C-reactive protein and lower blood pressure than a cereal-based diet in domestic pigs."[9]

Although this study used animal models, the findings suggest that a Palaeolithic diet might contribute to improved insulin sensitivity and reduced inflammation, both of which are important factors in managing chronic diseases in humans.

OMAD/intermittent/alternate day fasting

The 'One Meal a Day' diet is a fasting approach where individuals consume all their daily calories within a single meal, typically with a fasting window of twenty-three hours and an eating window of one hour.

Study 1: 'Effect of alternate-day fasting on weight loss, weight maintenance and cardioprotection among metabolically healthy obese adults: a randomized clinical trial'[10]

While not specifically focussed on OMAD, this study investigated alternate-day fasting, a form of intermittent fasting where participants alternated between days of normal eating and very low-calorie intake. The research found that intermittent fasting led to significant weight loss and improvements in cardiovascular risk factors.

Study 2: 'Intermittent fasting: the science of going without'[11]

This research provides an overview of various intermittent fasting regimens, including OMAD. It discusses the potential metabolic benefits of intermittent fasting, such as improved insulin sensitivity, reduced inflammation and enhanced cellular health.

Vegetarian Diet

The vegetarian diet is a plant-based eating pattern that excludes all animal products, focussing on fruits, vegetables, grains, legumes, nuts and seeds for nutrition.

Study 1: 'Mortality in vegetarians and comparable non-vegetarians in the United Kingdom'[12]

This large-scale study found that vegetarians had a 12 per cent lower risk of death compared to non-vegetarians.

Study 2: 'Position of the Academy of Nutrition and Dietetics: vegetarian diets'[13]

The paper highlights that vegetarians tend to have lower rates of obesity, heart disease, high blood pressure, type 2 diabetes and certain cancers. It also emphasizes that appropriately planned vegetarian diets are suitable for individuals during all life stages, including pregnancy, lactation, infancy and adolescence.

∼

Now that we have shown you the benefits of various types of diets, can you decide which one is the best? No? Then let's confuse you further by delving into the downsides of each of these diets.

Ketogenic Diet

Study 1: 'Effect of a ketogenic diet on the nutritional parameters of obese patients: a systematic review and meta-analysis'[14]

Many participants struggled with the sustainability of the diet due to its restrictiveness, leading to nutrient deficiencies and a higher risk of developing cardiovascular issues over time. The study concluded that while the ketogenic diet might offer short-term benefits, its long-term sustainability and potential adverse effects should be carefully considered.

Study 2: 'Impact of ketogenic diet on kidney health: a review of clinical and animal studies'[15]

The findings revealed that the high intake of animal proteins and fats, common in the ketogenic diet, could put a strain on the kidneys, potentially leading to impaired renal function and an increased risk of kidney stones.

Carnivore Diet

Study 1: 'Nutritional and health effects of the carnivorous zero-carb diet in health and disease'[16]

The study highlighted concerns about the lack of essential nutrients like fibre, vitamins and phytonutrients in an all-meat diet. Nutritional deficiencies could lead to adverse health effects, including an increased risk of nutrient-related diseases and compromised gut health due to the absence of dietary fibre.

Study 2: 'Impact of carnivorous diet on human oral and gut microbiome composition'[17]

The research found that the absence of dietary fibre and plant-based compounds in the carnivore diet led to significant changes in the gut microbiome composition.

Palaeo Diet

Study 1: 'Effect of increased physical activity on fructose-induced glycaemic response in healthy individuals'[18]

The diet was high in saturated fats, which could potentially increase the risk of cardiovascular diseases in the long term.

Study 2: 'Long-term effects of a Palaeolithic-type diet in obese postmenopausal women: a two-year randomized trial'[19]

While the diet led to initial improvements in weight and metabolic markers, the study found that adherence to the diet waned over time. Additionally, the researchers observed a decrease in bone mineral density among participants following the Palaeolithic-type diet.

OMAD Diet

Study 1: 'Meal frequency and timing in health and disease'[20]

While intermittent fasting diets, including OMAD, are mentioned as potential strategies for weight management, this review highlights concerns about extreme fasting durations. Prolonged fasting periods can lead to nutrient deficiencies and disrupt normal metabolic processes, potentially impacting energy levels and overall well-being.

Study 2: 'Impact of prolonged fasting on the risk of type 2 diabetes'[21]

The research found that individuals who engaged in prolonged nightly fasting intervals (including fasting for eighteen hours or more) had an increased risk of developing diabetes compared to those with shorter fasting intervals. This suggests that extended fasting periods, such as those practiced in OMAD, might have adverse effects on metabolic health.

Vegetarian Diet

Study 1: 'Nutrient intake and health status of vegetarians'[22]

The research found that while vegetarians tend to have lower intake of saturated fats and cholesterol, they may be at risk of certain nutritional deficiencies, particularly vitamin B12, iron, calcium, zinc and omega-3 fatty acids. These deficiencies can lead to anaemia, osteoporosis, and other health issues if not appropriately addressed through diet or supplementation.

Study 2: 'Bone health in vegetarians'[23]

The research highlighted that while vegetarians tend to have a lower risk of osteoporosis due to lower protein and calcium intake, they might still be at risk of bone fractures due to lower bone mineral density.

Now, based on these downsides, can you decide which is the worst diet? Still no?

~

We now have two studies each that show the upsides and downsides of certain diets, and we hope you are confused. We left it at two studies to reduce the level of confusion; we could've easily have cherry picked the data and confused you even more by adding five studies for each diet's upsides and downsides.

Typically, we will find a follower of one type of nutrition plan focussing on only the upsides while highlighting downsides of another plan to disincentivize a client or potential client.

The point is that there are merits to each diet, but one needs to find a diet they are going to stick with for a very long period of time, and do what works best for them with careful introspection. A lot of data in today's day and age is cherry picked and used by one person to show the superiority of one diet over another.

Diet is being packaged in gift-wraps, around similar concepts, with the same end goal of improving a person's health.

The problem that individuals face is that they try to pick out a nutrition plan without identifying whether they can stick to this one plan for decades.

As we explain in a later chapter on delayed gratification, once the novelty of a certain diet wears off, the individual moves to the next one, and this goes on in an endless cycle with the hope of finding the perfect diet.

In the opening chapter, I (Ankush) had mentioned how the low carb diet did not work sustainably for me so switching to a moderate carb high protein diet is what has worked for my process. I followed the low carb diet purely based on studies I read and success stories I saw and that caused me to make a biased decision that it would work for me. Mihir shared his personal story on how changing his lifestyle through calorie management helped him.

Each diet has its own merit and place, but that does not mean that one is superior to another.[24]

I jokingly term this biased form of analysis as 'poha analysis', let me explain why with an example:

Poha, also called pohe or chiwda or flattened rice, is a nutritious breakfast option rich in carbohydrates, iron and fibre, providing sustained energy throughout the day. Its quick cooking time and versatility make it an ideal choice for busy mornings, offering convenience without compromising on health.

Most consumers of the poha would find solace in this copy-pasted textbook definition as enough evidence to eat this as a healthy food item.

However, this definition provides no context for each individual's metabolic profile. Also, I (Ankush) just copy-pasted this definition from ChatGPT. Now that I've told you that I have simply copy-pasted a definition, you'll not be convinced so easily and will want to know more, right?

But let's say you followed this definition, that poha is good for busy mornings, and ate it on an empty stomach. The resultant impact on my blood sugar would be this via my glucose monitor:

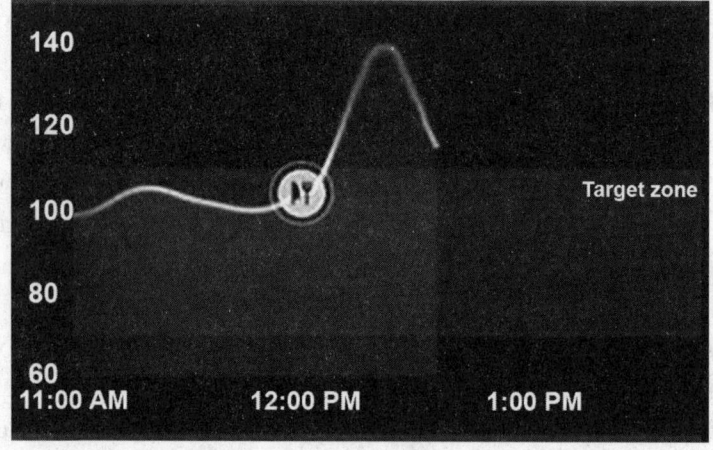

If I continued to do this, I could eventually have higher blood sugar and elevated insulin levels in the longer term if I kept having it on a regular basis.

The CGM gave me great insights that what fits for someone else may not necessarily fit for me.

The Investment Aspect

I observed the same logic being applied to investment strategies. There is no inherently better or worse strategy—each has its place in a portfolio. However, investors often assert superiority and selectively present data to demonstrate the effectiveness of one strategy over another, cherry picking performance metrics to their advantage.

Whenever a value strategy outperforms a growth strategy, critics attack growth strategies, and vice versa. This phenomenon is commonplace in the investment field, and Twitter (now X) serves as the prime platform for these debates.

Each investment plan possesses its own merits and place; this doesn't necessarily imply that one is inherently superior to another.

Notable figures such as Jim Simmons, Warren Buffett, Rakesh Jhunjhunwala, Radhakishan Damani, Stanley Druckenmiller and George Soros exemplify various successful investment approaches. All these names are doyens of the investment world who did not have the same set of processes when it came to investing, but each focussed on their own process and style and adhered to it for decades. Each was highly successful in his own right.

So, an investor should take into account the probabilities involved in each style of investing, just as they should with a nutrition plan.

The end goal of investing is to generate the highest returns one can by choosing a process that one can adhere to for decades without having to worry about their sleep.

This snippet from the *SageOne Knowledge Series Investment Newsletter* breaks down two styles of investing.[25]

Factor	Option 1	Option 2
Time Horizon	Long Term (3+ years), low churn	Short/Medium Term (1 day–2 years), high churn
Targeted Return	Similar to Nifty (12-15% CAGR)	Significant Alpha to Nifty (20-25% CAGR)
No of companies	Concentrated (2-10 companies)	Diversified (15-40 companies)
Focus Area	Business Quality – Great company	Valuation/Technical factors – Great stock
Type of Company	Compounder companies	Cyclical companies
Research Method	Focus on Qualitative aspects	Focus on Quantitative Aspects
Source of Idea	Own Research	Networking with other market participants

Source: SageOne Knowledge Series

Observing the two buckets, the process differs between long-term and short/medium-term approaches in terms of the parameters that investors consider. This discrepancy can also be attributed to variations between fundamental investing and technical investing.

Fundamental investing looks at the company's financial performance and expectations of it, and tries to come to a conclusion for an investment thesis. Technical investing largely ignores the financial performance and looks more at the price and trends, as per technical trends.

As history has shown, the second option makes sense for full-time investment professionals, and if you are a full-time working professional reading this, you may be better off entrusting your money to these professionals. The first option, on the other hand, has demonstrated a higher probability of yielding greater returns over the long term for both professional and retail investors, so it makes sense to consider this option if you are a full-time professional. However, it's essential to acknowledge that investors can also make serious mistakes in this process of choosing Option 1 too.

There is a third option, the passive option, which involves investing into a product which simply mimics the underlying index of the stock market, also known as index investing. This works best for someone who does not have the ability to choose option 1 and option 2, or does not have an adviser who can help them pick a fund that could possibly beat the index—which is a hard task to do. For such people, it could be wise to go for the passive investing option.

	Good outcome	Bad Outcome
Good process	Deserved Success	Bad Break
Bad process	Dumb Luck	Poetic Justice

Source: SageOne Knowledge Series

Another excellent example mentioned in the same newsletter is James Montier's highlight from *The Little Book of Behavioural Investing*, which states that most investments are based on speculative instincts and tips.[26] In the short term, dumb luck can blind the investor, and eventually, they may have to endure poetic justice. However, it is only through this learning phase that they discover the best process they can adhere to achieve deserved success.

This chart by Howard Marks in his investment letter for 2006 further backs Montier's points.[27]

	Conventional Behaviour	Unconventional Behaviour
Favorable Outcomes	Average good results	Above average results
Unfavorable Outcomes	Average bad results	Below average results

The chart highlights the fact that the greatest investors are often those who have held slightly unconventional views. It is through this unconventional thinking that they have achieved above-average results over long periods, making them outliers of success. However, this does not discount the massive wealth that conventional behaviour can generate over time, as we observed in the chapter on the power of compounding.

In my (Ankush's) own journey of working in the fund management industry, I have seen investors applaud our fund when our style of investing has worked across a particular time frame and then begin to envy another strategy over a different period that follows a different style that has probably outperformed our fund.[28]

There are typically two styles of fundamental investing:

Value Investing

This involves buying a stock whose price is depressed because it does not reflect the true value of the underlying business or its future potential.

Growth Investing

This involves buying a stock whose price may already reflect the current growth prospects of the business, even though it may be trading at a relatively higher price multiple. However, the business in the underlying stock is expected to continue its pace of growth and probably grow even faster.

There are some styles of investors who like to buy and hold to create wealth with an investment horizon of ten years, while others like to rotate between sectors in three to five years. Both these sets of investors have made money as per the goals they set out with, and one has always made more than the other during a two-to-three-year cycle.

This chart and data by *Capitalmind*, made by Anoop Vijaykumar, encapsulates how sectors rotate in the markets:[29]

NIFTY Sector Returns

	₹100 Invested in 2009	₹100 Invested in 2014	₹100 Invested in 2021
NIFTY CONSUMER DURABLES	3001.1	797.0	156.5
NIFTY TRANSPORTATION & LOGISTICS	2517.8	558.9	232.4
NIFTY IT	2259.3	486.4	166.2
NIFTY AUTO	2189.3	406.7	217.7
NIFTY PRIVATE BANK	1451.9	415.9	132.8
NIFTY FMCG	1319.2	365.2	165.8
NIFTY HEALTHCARE	1088.0	322.5	161.5
NIFTY OIL & GAS	1015.2	575.9	214.6
NIFTY PHARMA	883.5	261.4	148.2
NIFTY HOUSING	813.1	449.5	179.9
NIFTY COMMODITIES	698.4	427.4	222.5
NIFTY CPSE	440.1	436.0	373.8
NIFTY PSU BANK	412.3	281.2	391.6
NIFTY INFRASTRUCTURE	372.5	368.4	223.8
NIFTY REALTY	309.1	485.2	273.4
NIFTY MEDIA	280.5	130.7	129.5

Capitalmind Analysis. Total Returns include dividends. Data Source: niftyindices.com

Source: Capitalmind data as of February 2024.

Money rotates across sectors during different periods. While multiplier money is typically generated over the long term, certain styles of investors have successfully rotated between sectors. Even though certain sectors appear to have generated multiplier wealth over a ten-plus year period, only a handful of investors would typically have managed to hold on through the journey.

Cyclical funds and stocks will make supernormal returns over three-to-four-year periods but when compared to funds and stocks in less cyclical and more structural businesses, the returns for the latter style of investing could probably generate higher returns.

It is also impossible to predict whether the same trend that we see in terms of sectors that have given the highest returns over a ten-year period will be the same or change.

It's important to note that this is not an investment recommendation; rather, it's an illustration of how money shifts across various sectors. Investors of different styles may have outperformed others over these varying periods due to the ebbs and flows of the markets and sectors of the economy.

We'll often notice trending tweets and Instagram reels focussing on sectors currently in vogue in the market. Clients may express regret for not having invested in these sectors, which are not currently in their portfolio.

This phenomenon is common among the clients I work with, and I'm certain readers in the industry would encounter similar situations with their clients. It's part and parcel of human psychology, where envy comes into play when investing. Clients may begin to envy another strategy when it appears to be performing better than their current one, leading to an endless cycle of comparison.

We live in a world with plenty of choices. Decision fatigue is real—whether it's something as banal as choosing what food to order, what movie or web series to watch, or something more important like deciding on an investing strategy or a diet plan. We are inundated with choices, more than we want and far more than we need.

And if decision fatigue doesn't get us, then FOMO will. We'll see others doing better because they've chosen differently to us. We'll have the urge to shift from what we're doing to what someone else is doing, even before rationally gauging whether our current approach is yielding results.

The goal of whichever path we take—investing or nutrition—should essentially lead us to the same destination, as per our goals. All we have to do is pick a path that works for us and doesn't disrupt our sleep. Some paths may be faster for some people than for others.

When it comes to our investing journey, the ultimate aim is to build wealth or, in simpler terms, make money. And how do we do that?

We buy low and sell high.

The process of reaching the low and the high will be different for each individual. While it sounds awfully simple, as we know, this is not the case. It takes years of patience, research and fortitude. But essentially, it comes down to the crux of buying low, selling high, and making money.

In fact, financial journalist Jason Zweig, in one of his blogs, perfectly captures the essence of all investment writing, investing and possibly even this book, 'My job is to write the exact same thing between fifty and 100 times a year in such a way that neither my editors nor my readers will ever think I am repeating myself.'

In investing too, there are different ways to say the same thing, but the end goal is to make money.

When it comes to our fitness journey, we essentially want to be healthy by having our essential metabolic markers in line. If we can adhere to the processes and basic parameters to track, which we mentioned previously in the opening chapter, we can broadly expect to be healthy over the long term.

Each style would be uniquely suited to an individual based on their preferences and life circumstances, but the end goal of each style remains the same—health and wealth.

Key Principles Learned from This Chapter

- The key goal is to be healthy and wealthy, and each person is free to choose their set of processes to achieve these goals.
- One style or process being good does not mean that other process should be deemed bad or not useful.
- The method we choose should be sustainable over decades.

9

Reverse Compounding

We've talked previously about how the principle of compounding yields gradual growth when proactive measures are taken. However, a contrasting force also operates, leading to a gradual decline if appropriate measures are neglected. This is called reverse compounding, and it is as dark and gloomy as compounding is bright and sunny.

Reverse compounding quietly infiltrates our health and wealth through two phenomena:

Inflation, the silent degradation of our wealth.

Sarcopenia, the silent degradation of our health.

In the same way that our money degrades in value when we do not put it to effective use, our body does too.

What Does Inflation Mean?

Let's begin by defining the root cause of wealth erosion, that is, inflation. Inflation refers to the general increase in the prices of goods and services in an economy over time, resulting in the decline in the purchasing power of a currency.

In other words, inflation means that the same amount of money can buy fewer goods and services in the following years than before. Inflation is usually measured as the percentage increase in the overall price level of a basket of goods and services, typically calculated over a period of one year. Inflation can be caused by various factors, including increases in the money supply, rising production costs, changes in consumer demand and global economic factors.

For example, let's assume that a packet of milk, currently priced at Rs 100, will cost Rs 150 in the next five years. Let's also assume that this packet of milk constitutes 1 per cent of your total monthly expenses, and that your monthly salary is Rs 10,000.

Now, five years later, even though the price of milk has increased by 50 per cent, let's say your salary has only grown by 30 per cent. Today, the milk packet will account for 1.2 per cent of your total monthly expenses, slowly eating into your monthly income.

This expense will gradually become a more significant part of your monthly budget, and the cost of milk is just one of many expenses you have each month, which will also have gone up in the interim.

For many of us, the rate of salary increase may be limited based on our job profiles as well, and there are certain expenses which we may not be able to avoid.

Moving beyond the milk packet to larger, goal-based expenditures, we see an even gloomier picture.

In a *moneycontrol.com* article titled 'If you're a father, you're old enough to start saving for your kid's education', an important point was brought up—that education inflation has led to a rise in costs.[2]

Reverse Compounding

'The interesting trend to note is that education inflation has been 10–12 per cent over the years, which is double that of household inflation,' the article quotes Tivesh Shah, founder of Tru-Worth Finsultants, as saying. 'A great example of this could be the MBA programme from IIM Bangalore. The cost of an MBA last decade was close to Rs 13 lakh, but is now well over Rs 23 lakh for a two-year programme.'

The Rise and Rise of Education Costs

- Education Expenses Include Tuition Fees, Accommodation Costs, and Other Components
- Expenditure on Education rising with the Growth of Private Institutions
- Education Likely to Become Unaffordable without a Financial Plan in place

Degree	2022 - Present	2038 - Projected
Engineering	Rs. 12,00,000	Rs. 61,00,000
MBBS	Rs. 50,00,000	Rs. 2,53,00,000

Source: Article titled 'If you're a father, you're old enough to start saving for your kid's education' on moneycontrol.com

Source: moneycontrol.com[2]

So the question is, how do salaried individuals combat these rises in costs? We provided the answer in the opening chapter—investing in an asset class which has the best potential to cover these costs over the longer term, preferably equity.

Equities and the 40-year Outperformance

Over the past 40 years, Equities have delivered higher returns than all other asset classes

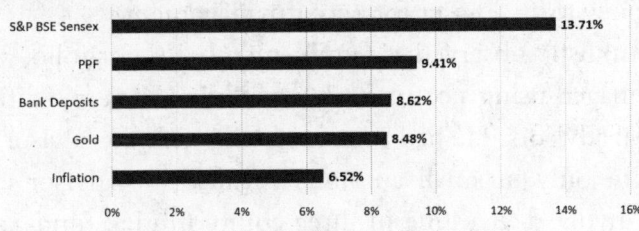

- S&P BSE Sensex: 13.71%
- PPF: 9.41%
- Bank Deposits: 8.62%
- Gold: 8.48%
- Inflation: 6.52%

Source: Article titled 'Equity beats gold, PPF, bank FD! Stocks delivered best returns over 40 years' on zeebiz.com

(Pre taxes-post taxes bank deposits trend lower than inflation)
Source: Zeebiz.com[3]

This chart highlights how the forty-year return of equity as an asset class has protected capital over inflation. While past returns are not indicative of the future, equity generally has the highest chance of beating inflation over long periods of time. These historical price performances do not represent the future, but what we can learn from history is that equity typically has the highest probability of protecting our money from these rises in costs.

Mind you, the journey of wealth creation, as with anything else, requires an investor to have the ability to withstand significant fluctuations in the portfolio.

Thinking of market volatility as a fee rather than a penalty is an important aspect of developing the mindset that allows us to remain invested long enough for investments to work in our favour, at the cost of repeating what we mentioned in the third chapter, 'Less Is More'.

Most Indians are not able to reap the benefits of this asset class as they are not willing to treat short-term pains in the market as a learning fee but rather as a punishment.

For individual stock-pickers, there may be cases where stocks have significantly outperformed or underperformed inflation. This depends on the amount of time we dedicate to researching a stock. If we don't have the time to do so, we should entrust our money to an adviser for better management.

I (Ankush) observed a family member's portfolio, which was managed using a combination of advice from two different financial advisors. He had been investing with the advisor since 2015 but only in small amounts because the advisor's plan, which involved investing in three equity mutual funds, didn't seem exciting enough. So, he decided to allocate only Rs 5,000 out of his planned monthly investment of Rs 50,000.

Later, he met another advisor who presented a more enticing plan. This plan involved regularly investing in six to seven stocks each month to potentially boost returns.

The second advisor showcased the ten-year track record of these stocks, which captivated the investor. As a result, he decided to allocate the other Rs 45,000 to this new strategy.

Fast forward to 2023, the seemingly 'boring' mutual fund portfolio has generated an impressive 11.5 per cent compound annual growth rate (CAGR) return for the investor, while the stock portfolio has yielded a mere 2.6 per cent CAGR return, which is weaker than the rate of growth of inflation, thereby defeating the entire purpose of investing into those stocks.

Most people are not good when it comes to making an individual portfolio of stocks, but the thrill is something that most cannot control dabbing into.

When it comes to consistency, it literally pays dividends not to be lured by flashy returns, as we have emphasized before.[4]

What Does Sarcopenia Mean?

Now that we have learned how to protect our capital against depreciation, does it not make sense to protect our bodies against depreciation as well, ensuring that we can enjoy the fruits of our labour accumulated over a lifetime?

Just as keeping our money in a savings account for extended periods or investing in the wrong asset classes can erode our wealth, neglecting exercise or investing time in improper forms of nutrition and exercise can lead to a gradual erosion of our health.

This phenomenon is known as sarcopenia, and it is defined as the age-related loss of muscle mass and function.[5] But this can be slowed down drastically with the help of effective training and nutrition.

Sarcopenia is a silent killer of health. Every single individual reading this chapter is living with this 'disease', as is everyone else, and most people aren't even aware of it. In fact, even some people in the health and wellness space are not aware of it.

The natural ageing process causes a gradual decline in muscle mass and strength, which begins around the age of thirty and slowly starts to take a toll on our bodies. According to the Harvard Medical School, after age thirty, most people lose 3–5 per cent of their muscle mass per decade.[6]

Two fundamental symptoms of sarcopenia resulting from our neglect at an early age are:
1. Shrinkage of nerve cells in the brain responsible for and involved in transmitting signals to initiate muscle movement, which could contribute to age-related lethargy.
2. Reduced levels of growth hormone due to insufficient nutrition, sleep and exercise.

The most common symptom of sarcopenia is muscle loss and weakness. Additional symptoms may include:
1. Decreased stamina.
2. Difficulty in performing daily activities.
3. Slower walking pace.
4. Challenges in climbing stairs.
5. Poor balance and an increased risk of falls.
6. Reduction in muscle size.

These issues are a result of muscle loss and tend to manifest later in life, highlighting the importance of addressing sarcopenia early through proper nutrition and exercise.

We often blame it on age, but the depreciation of our body over time is not just due to that but also due to the lack of maintenance.

You may ask, why is muscle mass important? Just to clarify—by muscle mass, we do not mean that you have to build bulging biceps or a massive body. We are referring to muscle mass that allows us to live a life that does not lead to issues in the future.

Muscle mass is crucial, particularly as we age, for several key reasons.

First, it plays a vital role in maintaining overall physical function and mobility. Muscles allow us to perform everyday activities like walking, standing and lifting objects.

Second, muscle mass is closely linked to metabolism. Muscle tissue requires more energy to maintain than fat, so having more muscle can help boost our metabolic rate. This means that maintaining or increasing muscle mass can aid in weight management and reduce the risk of obesity and related health conditions, such as type 2 diabetes.

Third, muscle mass is essential for preserving bone health. Muscles pull on bones during physical activities, which stimulates bone density. This helps prevent conditions like osteoporosis, which is more prevalent in older individuals.

Fourth, muscle mass can contribute to improved quality of life by enhancing our ability to perform daily tasks independently and participate in activities we enjoy.

Sarcopenia has been associated with a number of negative health outcomes and diseases, including:

Falls and Fractures

Reduced muscle strength and function are associated with an increased risk of these in older adults. A study published in the *Journal of the American Geriatrics Society* found that sarcopenia was a risk factor for falls in older men and women.[7] A fall increased the chances of 15–30 per cent of these individuals dying within twelve months of the fall.

Disability and Loss of Independence

A study published in the *Journal of the American Geriatrics Society* found that sarcopenia was associated with an increased risk of disability in activities of daily living.[8]

Cardiovascular Disease

A study published in the *Journal of the American College of Cardiology* found that low muscle mass was associated with an increased risk of cardiovascular events in older adults.[9]

Diabetes

A study published in the *Journal of Diabetes and its Complications* found that sarcopenia was associated with an increased risk of developing type 2 diabetes in older adults.[10]

Cancer

Sarcopenia has been associated with an increased risk of cancer and poorer outcomes in cancer patients. A study published in the *Journal of Cachexia, Sarcopenia and Muscle* found that sarcopenia was associated with a higher risk of mortality in cancer patients.[11]

We don't mean to give you heart palpitations with these statistics and studies, but want to open your eyes to the possibilities of not combating this issue of building adequate muscle for the future.

Sarcopenia is not as linear as inflation in a mathematical sense—it can impact individuals well before old age too, if lifestyle is not kept in check. The same way, inflation can wreck an individual's wealth in the future if they don't keep their spend in check.

Dr Peter Attia has written an article in which he has interpreted various studies on how muscle mass and strength are so important as we age.[12] 'If you have the aspiration of kicking ass when you're eighty-five, you can't afford to be average when you're fifty.'

The only basis for this by having adequate muscle mass. And it's never too late to do so, as we saw with the example of Ankush's father Ajit Datar in chapter four.

Solutions to Sarcopenia

Here are the basic solutions for sarcopenia offered by science.

Resistance Training

Also known as strength training, this is mandatory to ensure that we do not lose muscle mass as we age. There are various forms of resistance training:

a. *Weight training:* This involves using external weights, such as dumbbells and barbells, to perform exercises that target specific muscle groups, providing a versatile and functional approach to strength development by engaging stabilizing muscles.

b. *Bodyweight training:* This relies on using one's own body weight for resistance in exercises like push-ups, squats and pull-ups, promoting functional strength, flexibility and endurance without the need for additional equipment.

c. *Resistance bands:* These are elastic bands that provide resistance in various exercises, accommodating different fitness levels and allowing for portable and versatile strength training routines that emphasize both concentric and eccentric muscle contractions.

With each form of exercise, one can use the principles from the chapter on the power of compounding to improve their level in a slow incremental fashion. Conventional wisdom tells us to slow down as we age and not to visit the gym or lift weights, but the reverse is true. A 2012 study showed that among inactive individuals, ten weeks of resistance training helped increase lean muscle mass by 1.4 kg, reduce body fat by 1.8 kg and increase resting metabolic rate by 7 per cent.[13] The study also pointed out that strength training helped to reduce LDL cholesterol and triglycerides, and increase HDL cholesterol.

Protein

This is the building block for muscle in the body and the most important macronutrient. The body breaks protein down into amino acids, which it uses to build muscle. However, older individuals often experience a phenomenon called anabolic resistance, which lowers their bodies' ability to break down and synthesize protein.

Therefore, as we begin resistance training at an older age, we may need more protein.

The recommended levels of protein are 0.8 g of protein per kg of bodyweight for inactive individuals. Active individuals carrying out progressive resistance training would require 1-1.3 g of protein per kg of bodyweight. This means if you weigh 70 kilos, the minimum amount of protein you would require is 70–90 grams.

~

Most individuals of past generations quit investing in the stock market due to the psychological trauma of having lost money. They even call it a form of 'gambling'. However, it's clear they did not have efficient processes in place.

In the chapter on compounding, we spoke about the 'flywheel effect' as explained by Jim Collins in his masterpiece *Good to*

Great.[14] There is another concept in the book called the Doom Loop effect, which ties in to reverse compounding.

The Doom Loop occurs among those people who push the flywheel in one direction for a certain period of time; then, seeing how long it takes for the wheel to gain momentum, they will stop it, change course and send it in a new direction; then stop, change course and send it another direction, and so on.

This hampers the most important rule of compounding—to not interrupt it unnecessarily.

This Doom Loop plays out in real life in the following ways in health and wealth too:
1. We start a specific diet or exercise plan; we do it for some time and don't see the results; so, we change course and find the next best plan. This goes on as an endless cycle.
2. We start investing in a fund or a stock; we don't see the desired results in our stipulated time period; we change course and find the next best plan to give us faster returns. This goes on as an endless cycle.

Inflation and Sarcopenia: A Double Whammy

Having explained inflation and sarcopenia, we should point out that having both these problems later in life can lead to disaster.

Muscle is the insurance corpus we build to help us against long-term disease, by paying the premium of showing up regularly for workouts; just as we regularly pay health insurance premiums for an insurance corpus against health hazards. This is called real-life asset allocation.

We lose money in health insurance if we stay healthy, and gain money if we fall sick. But the smart person focusses on maintaining health, not winning or losing money.

Typically, a person who does not have inflation-beating returns in their portfolio and follows a lifestyle of poor health is going to face a double whammy in the future.

Sarcopenia is also a growing concern in healthcare. In fact, a systematic review in 2017 from a study comparing healthcare costs between sarcopenic and non-sarcopenic patients found that healthcare costs were significantly higher in sarcopenic patients.[15] The study, conducted on patients from the United States, highlighted the importance of early detection and intervention for sarcopenia to reduce healthcare costs and improve patient outcomes.

While we are not propagating a public healthcare policy here, these statistics should make individuals understand that not taking care of health early on could have a significant bearing on the cost they may need to incur in the future.

A great way to avoid reverse compounding, although it is much easier said than done, is to imagine ourselves physically and financially ten years down the line from today.

Ask yourself, in ten years, do I want to be able to comfortably bend my back, or do I want to be able to run five kilometres comfortably, without panting for breath? In ten years, do I want to be able to easily take a foreign holiday every year without having to worry too much about my finances?

We should take a long-term view, because it works in terms of goal-setting. In fact, a study showed that individuals were likely to value the future more when a specific date was set to achieve a goal, such as 'I want to buy a house by 10 August 2033'.[16] Keeping a specific date added more incentive for people to work better towards a goal, rather than 'I want to buy a house in ten years.'

For example, Ankush's long-term lifting goals have allowed him to work efficiently towards his process. By 20 January 2024, he wanted to bench press six reps of 100 kilos, and he wanted to run a half-marathon in under one hour and thirty-five minutes. With a well-defined process, he was able to achieve both goals.

The SIP calculators of many financial services firms work wonderfully in that way—we can find out how much we can roughly earn on a specific day in ten years if we follow the SIP process at a set rate of return.[17]

The Greek myth of Odysseus (also known by the Latin form of the name, Ulysses) is often used a case in point. He was a king who was captaining a ship across the seas, and skirted the island of the Sirens—human-like beings with alluring voices that were known to lead sailors to their ruin. So, Ulysses told his crew to plug their ears with wax and instructed them to tie him to the ship's mast, because he wanted to hear their song without moving towards his ruin. This has come to be known in investing as the 'Ulysses contract'.

Unlike Ulysses, we have technology today to keep our health and wealth in check by using restrictions and blockers. There are also unique ways one can use to be disciplined and avoid habits that could reverse the process of compounding—and lead us astray like the Sirens' song.

In fact, a study titled 'Tying Odysseus to the Mast' showed how participants who had functions restricted in their bank accounts and had money automatically debited from their savings accounts increased their savings rate by 81 per cent.[18]

Another study showed participants who automatically set aside a part of their future salary increments increased their level of savings.[19] While this is basic common sense, it is surprising how few people do it. Asset management companies even have a tool where we can step up our SIP amount by a pre-fixed percentage assuming our salary increase; this helps one automatically continue investing more as the salary increases.

Healthy individuals often do this by keeping a restriction on food delivery apps on their phone, while participants of in stock market can avoid being influenced by daily market fluctuations by keeping blockers on their market-tracking apps.

The crux is that if we care about something, we will try to find ways to achieve that goal. Creating good financial habits early on in life is the key to achieve our goals.

In the United States, there is a programme known as child development accounts, designed for long-term investment objectives.[20] This programme offers new parents automated savings procedures, including deposits, savings targets and notifications from universities, all aimed at securing their children's future.

The Indian government's Sukanya scheme for girl children provides similar financial security for daughters, with payouts at college age and marriageable age.

Ultimately, parents are the ones building the child's financial foundation, and everyone involved is united in this early commitment.

Similarly, on the health front, creating good habits early on in life is important to reverse the impact that a lack of exercise can have on our lives.

A study by epidemiologist Dr Ralph Paffenbarger followed 17,000 Harvard alumni, because these were successful people stuck in a time-crunch due to their busy schedules.[21] The widespread study involved questioning all parameters, including lifestyle habits, smoking, drinking, and most importantly, exercise. All of these people had similar hours and stress at work, but the individuals who began exercising in their twenties, thirties or even their forties, showed a 20 per cent lower rate of death during their fifties, and a 50 per cent lower death rate during their sixties and beyond.

Exercise actually gets more and more important, but the caveat is that we need to start taking charge today.

What kind of exercise we choose, and what instrument of investing we choose, is important.

Key Principles Learned from This Chapter

- Inevitably, our health and wealth go into reverse gear if we do not make a process to slow down reverse compounding.
- This is a lifelong journey and applicable across all ages.
- Being consistent does not mean anything if we are being consistent with the wrong process. In this scenario, compounding ends up working in reverse.

10

Delayed Gratification

Ranveer Malhotra is a young corporate professional a few years into his career, earning a handsome salary that sustains a luxurious lifestyle.

Every month, he spends all his earnings on expensive clothes and indulges in fancy dinners almost every other night. By the time he has spent his salary, the month ends and the next salary is credited, and the cycle repeats. He also loves to flaunt his lifestyle on Instagram, and his friends and family look at him enviously.

He has no time to maintain his health, and in any case, no one is going to envy him for how healthy he is, so he just ignores that aspect of his life. He focusses on what brings him status in society.

After many years of this lifestyle, his wife, probably the only person in his life not bothered by his show of vanity, asks, 'Ranveer what have you planned for our retirement?'

He is dumbstruck by this question. Then, he starts to allocate a certain amount of money from his monthly income to his savings, in the hopes of being able to answer his wife's question next time with a straight face.

But this is frustrating, as he does not have all the money he wants every month to sustain his lavish lifestyle.

This reduction in spending power means he is invited to fewer social gatherings than before.

This makes him depressed because he always tried to chase status and did the most fashionable things.

All the years of living lavishly have left him with a protruding belly, which was a sign for him to get healthy. But now, he has developed a novel disease. He probably still doesn't realize that he hasn't even saved up enough money to live out the rest of his life comfortably.

Back in the day, Ranveer thought he would miss out on life in his youth by wasting time, saving money and working on his health. It seemed like an opportunity cost for him. But today, he is bearing the actual cost of the short-term pain that he avoided.

Is he late? Absolutely not, but tempering expectations is going to be really hard for him after years of living a certain way.

The science behind this hypothetical case is that Ranveer's dopamine levels have been elevated to a certain baseline, which means not having all the money and time he needed to do the fun things he wanted to do is making him feel unfulfilled. This is akin to getting off an addictive substance—his level of dopamine or expectation for that substance or lifestyle is so elevated that it is going to take time for his body to neurologically adapt and bring down expectations to a new baseline.

If you remember from our explanation of dopamine, the more we consume an addictive substance, the more of that substance we need the next time. Neuroadaptation of our body to habits can work for us or against us.

Behavioural economist Anne Bretteville-Jensen conducted an experiment with heroin and amphetamine addicts, along with ex-users of the drugs. The participants had to imagine they had a winning lottery ticket worth 100,000 Norwegian kroner, or about US$14,600, and were asked whether they would rather have less money right now or the full amount later. Surprisingly, the active drug users wanted it now, while the ex-users and non-users did not accept the loss.

Delaying gratification does not mean giving up enjoyment and living a life of despair. It means being cognizant of one's goals by making a little sacrifice today for a better tomorrow.

All valuable things in life come at the expense of some form of sacrifice; there are no free lunches in life.

But our hypothetical Ranveer is not alone in coming to a moment of realization later in life—a study by Max Life showed nine in ten Indians regret not starting their retirement planning process early.[1] It also found that 80 per cent of urban Indians believe they will be in good health post-retirement, with 58 per cent opting for preventive health check-ups in the last three years and 40 per cent seeking annual check-ups. We suspect that out of the 80 per cent who believe they will be in good health, a large portion would not actually be in good health right now, let alone in their old age.

The reason they postpone their future planning is a phenomenon in economics called 'delay discounting'—we value what we have today more than something very far off in the future, and the value goes down the longer we have to wait for it.

Take your time and think about this one: would you prefer ten lakh rupees today or one paisa doubling every day for thirty days?

Money to be received in the future has a lesser value for us psychologically, a 2005 study showed.² This is an example of time inconsistency—even though we know the option later in the future will benefit us, we tend to move towards the shorter, more easily available option.³

Case in point, the value of that paisa doubling every day over thirty days would be Rs 53,68,709.12. Read that again. Over Rs 53 lakh, instead of the Rs 10 lakh today you probably wanted to choose.

Choosing to allocate time to go to the gym, or declining social invitations from friends today may feel like sacrificing a small portion of the present, which appears to be a cost. Keeping a certain portion of money to invest today rather blowing it up on that shiny expensive object may seem like a lost opportunity. It can feel like a missed moment. But it doesn't have to be if we have defined our goals from the outset.

This is the nature of health too, and regrettably, given the opportunity, many of us would prefer to spend that hour elsewhere rather than working on improving our fitness levels.

Most people don't feel the urge to take out that one hour of the day to exercise, just like most people don't feel like going to their jobs every day for eight hours. But we do the latter regardless. Why? Because individuals are accountable to their employers to justify their salary, and accountable to themselves to ensure they are able to provide a decent living for their families.

Allocating that half hour or one hour to focus on health becomes difficult for them because they have not defined their health goals and have no accountability.

Defining a goal in the future allows us to delay gratification, and ensures that we can create a process that does not rely us spending time purely on willpower.

We may notice this process when we work with a financial planner, who sits with us to create a plan to achieve a goal in the future; they are also subconsciously building the practice of delaying gratification for us by pulling out an allocation from our monthly income and deploying it into productive assets.

It's the same thing working with a nutritionist and fitness trainer, who each make us focus on what we can do by defining the objective.

The differences between the choices we make today versus tomorrow is that decisions today involve emotions, and decisions made for the future involve less of them. Short-term emotion and feelings of being 'in the moment' are among the biggest reasons for our inability to delay gratification.

A process in place allows us to get past emotion: setting a set date for SIPs, or setting days for specific workouts in the gym.

Being envious of someone else also impairs our ability to delay gratification. Do you see your favourite cricketer and the way they flash their expensive watches and lifestyle on Instagram? But we rarely ask what happens after their careers end, because we are so absorbed in today without thinking too much about tomorrow.

Professional athletes are a great example of individuals who have a short stint under the spotlight, but have to live a completely different reality when their careers come to an end. A 2015 study showed that 16 per cent of players in the US' National Football League (NFL) filed for bankruptcy after twelve years despite earning $3.2 million a year.[4] A 2009 article showed how 60 per cent of NBA players were in financial trouble within five years of retiring from the game.[5] According to another article, an estimated 40 per cent of soccer players also went broke within five years of retiring, and many more came under financial stress.[6]

These are also probably not the people we want to look up to for our health goals, because they are solely focussed on a single goal or event that they want to optimize for. A professional swimmer, for example, could be eating 10,000 calories a day today to work towards their current goal of an Olympic medal without worrying about how this will impact their health over the long term. In fact, many of these athletes would find it hard to use this same process of training and nutrition when they have retired.

Several athletes who were once the epitome of fitness face health issues when they retire, as their lifestyle was curated to meet certain goals in the short term and not for longevity—a fact which is often missed by many of us who envy them.

Exercise is the ultimate physical form of delayed gratification. It is immediately toxic to the cells, leading to increased temperatures, oxygen and glucose deprivation in the short term, during the movement. In fact, exercise literally involves tearing the muscles during movement and their subsequent recovery.

Yet, it is clear that there are tremendous long-term benefits to it.

Muscle takes time to build. We will go days, even weeks, seeing practically zero change, but we need to push past this phase if we want to see any growth.

The same goes with diet—fat loss takes time, and we can only safely lose around one or two pounds of weight a week on a sustainable basis. The faster we try to lose the pounds, the less consistent this process will be, and the faster we will jump back into the vicious cycle of putting on the weight.

Ankush's story

I take these principles of delaying gratification very religiously and apply them to my life in the case of weightlifting and running.

I had worked to get the 90 kg mark on my bench press in the gym after almost four years, gradually adding 0.5 or one kilo each time I worked out. I achieved this by subconsciously delaying gratification, without contemplating how, one day, I would be able to hit my goal of lifting 100 kg.

The trainers told me to rush in and just do 100 kg because the goal was right there. But I took three more weeks to get there, because if I had jumped straight up, I would have risked injury, which would have meant going all the way back down to 90 kg or even less, in order to rebuild the muscle. Please take this as a humble brag, but I am now probably one of three people in my gym who can comfortably bench press 100 kg, because I had accepted the fact that this goal would take me a considerable amount of time.

This holds true for any weight category, and is the reason why many individuals get bored of the rate of progress in the gym, try to go all in for heavier weights, and eventually fail and quit the entire process.

With running, I follow the same principle. This is a discipline where one can easily injure themselves if they push their body beyond preparation. I remember how battered my body got when I pushed through the last seven kilometres of the first full marathon I ran in 2017. My mind had convinced me that my one year of preparation would have gone to waste had I stopped at the thirty-five kilometre mark.

When we run a marathon, if we complete thirty-five kilometres, we have gained that much distance. However, the cognitive mind says we failed and didn't finish forty-two kilometres. If our body is physically not able to complete the remaining seven kilometres, it is okay to stop rather than break it.

It takes experience to accept a situation and to delay gratification for the next opportunity.

This chase for instant returns in investing and instant results in fitness and nutrition is why most people fail to remain consistent and burn out.

As author and decision-making guru Shane Parrish says, 'Most people can't do it consistently because they want instant gratification. They want to see the results right now. Just because the results aren't immediately visible doesn't mean they are not accumulating.'[7]

Delayed Gratification in Investing

Delayed gratification is one of the most powerful concepts one has to keep in mind when investing in stocks. Concentrating on chasing returns without considering valuations is a test of one's ability to delay gratification.

A great lesson on the principles of delaying gratification comes from the legendary investor Parag Parikh's book, *Value Investing and Behavioral Finance*, where he writes about one of India's most successful companies, Infosys.[8]

During the technology boom of 2000, most IT stocks were surging far ahead of their fundamentals, and Infosys was an example of a great company trading at absurd valuations. If you had bought Infosys in March 2000 at the peak of the IT boom when everything was rising because you felt a sense of FOMO, you would not have seen gains until June 2006. It's not like there was a lull in the markets—the Bombay Stock Exchange Sensex went to 21,000 in 2008 from 3,000 in 2003.

There have been many such instances in market history in different avatars, and our ability to delay gratification is a skill we will have to hone. Successful investing is about people having to agree with us, later.

We go back to Warren Buffett, who was able to go decades without buying stocks unless they came at a reasonable valuation. And buying stocks is his full-time profession. He had close to $163 billion sitting uninvested on his balance sheet in December 2023.[10]

Buffet is clear that he refuses to jump in with the rest of the herd because he has his clearly defined processes in place, and his track record speaks for itself.

Titan, one of India's most successful stories, is also a great case of delaying gratification. If we had invested Rs 1 lakh in Titan in 2008, then in fifteen years, by 2023, our investment would have grown to Rs 70 lakh.[11]

You would have had to go through unrealized losses of as high as 45 per cent in 2009, a fall of 31 per cent in 2010, 36 per cent in 2012 and 41 per cent in 2019. There were many more volatile periods which I excluded. This is the trend across almost all 'multibagger' stocks.

Most people are not able to stomach these downturns to achieve the end result.

This is not an investment recommendation on Titan; the idea is to show you that those who have done the work and have learnt from experience know that delaying gratification is part and parcel of the long-term investment process.

However, delaying gratification in a financial sense comes from a place of relative privilege too. Coming from a poorer background brings a level of stress on individuals, leading to poor financial decisions in the hope of getting out of their rut. This phenomenon is called the 'scarcity mindset', and occurs when the stress of an ongoing situation in our lives overpowers the way we think, and subsequently handle other situations.

Observe the individuals who get fooled for assured return products, 'ninja loans' or predatory loans—an extreme level of stress in their lives causes them to take these financial decisions.

A 2017 study on the population of Bangladesh showed how forgoing immediate rewards was difficult for lower income groups—a majority of the group chose to receive six dollars today instead of eighteen dollars after three months.[12] While this is one single study, there are multiple others highlighting this phenomenon through different patterns.

Delaying gratification becomes easier when we define our goals and not get greedy.

So, if you happen to be somebody who is not financially well off, don't put yourself under more stress by exposing yourself to the unsolicited advice of external parties and influencers. Work hard till you can see that you can set aside a piece of your income to invest. This is the boring but brutal truth for most of us.

Another interesting study done on Indian sugarcane farmers, based on Raven's Progressive Matrices test, showed how they reacted in terms of their cognitive capacity during financial stress.[13]

Prior to their harvest seasons, when they were feeling financially poorer, their IQ scores were 25 per cent lower. Post-harvest, when they were relaxed and had money coming in, their IQ scores were only 10 per cent lower than the baseline of Raven's Progressive Matrix IQ test.

In today's day and age, unlike our ancestors, we can instantly get away from boredom by scrolling on social media, ordering our favourite snack or trading our favourite stock at the click of a button.

But embracing boredom is a very important step in delaying gratification.

In the past, boredom was considered a curse; today, it is a luxury to be bored.

Based on our experiences, there are two broad types of boredom:[14]

Avoidable boredom, one that serves no purpose. This includes pausing a TV show, movie or book we are bored with, or anything related to entertainment.

Unavoidable boredom, which is part of many phases in our lives. However, this type of boredom leads to growth. Examples include:

1. Investing systematically for years without making any fancy changes.
2. Doing the same kind of workout for years, gradually increasing the weight, pace or number of repetitions each time.
3. Following the same meal plan to maintain our health over years.
4. Performing routine tasks at work that accumulate into something big.

Human beings are desirous of some level of novelty, and as soon as this wears off, boredom starts creeping in.

The key to consistency in an investing plan, exercise plan and work is getting past that boredom and novelty factor. Junk food provides a sense of novelty through its taste, as does the quest to find the next multibagger stock every other day, as does finding that thirty-day workout to get us ripped.

The most successful people around us, whom we admire, continue to engage in the same routine tasks every single day without complaining, and they have been doing so for years on end.

So, even though it is obvious to most of us that delaying gratification is going to help us, why do we keep running away from it?

Delayed Gratification

This can be explained by an invisible force of nature highlighted by American author Steven Pressfield, called 'resistance'.[15]

This is any action that rejects immediate short-term gratification in favour of long-term growth, health or integrity. It is the force of nature that every individual encounters.

Some activities in my (Ankush's) life that spring up resistance:

Resistance Training

It is called what it is for a reason—pushing beyond that resistance leads to real growth. It also serves as a reminder that we will never feel like showing up, but the real work is in just showing up; the rest will follow.

Work

Not every day at work will be exciting or enjoyable, but we have to show up regardless. Many exciting outcomes at work result from seemingly mundane tasks, such as consistently reading about an investee company, following up with clients, or performing routine operational work. We have to overcome the resistance in our mind to tackle the tasks that have been causing us worry.

Investing

There are moments when a stock or a fund, which has not performed for a period of time, induces a form of FOMO. Meanwhile, watching another fund or stock outpace our current investments can create a feeling of resistance within us, prompting thoughts that we should sell and allocate money elsewhere. It is essential to battle through these periods.

Most individuals who are consistently able to get beyond this resistance at work increase their probability of making wealth simply because they showed up more often for situations that needed them more than others. Of course, one can feel this resistance any time, but as we learn and embrace it, we start feeling its grip loosening.

While we are not advocates of technical analysis, interestingly enough, technical analysis also uses the term 'resistance'.

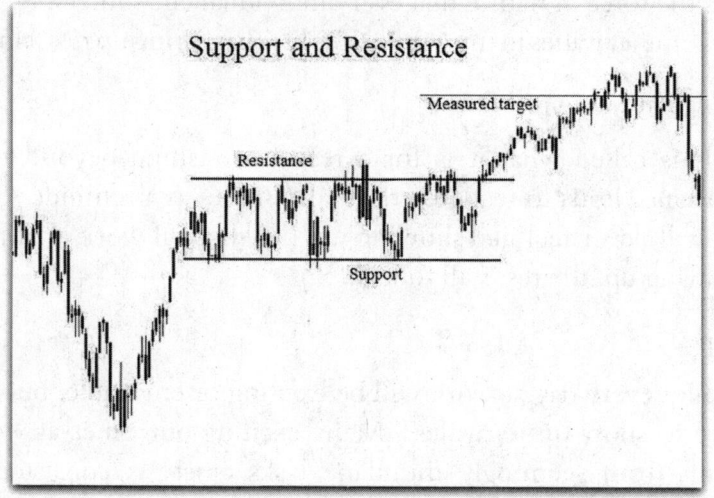

Source: Altfins.[16]

In stock-market terms, the value of a stock often encounters a critical point known as the line of resistance. When a stock crosses this line, it can lead to a breakout of resistance and a subsequent breakout or growth in the stock price.

Similarly, the value of a stock also encounters a point called 'support' in stock-market terms, below which the stock goes on a downward trend. The longer we delay, the more challenging it becomes to accomplish those tasks, eventually leading to a reduction in the probability of pursuing them.

Here's a simple chart Ankush had put on his door as a reminder of the principles of delayed gratification in fitness and investing:

Delayed Gratification

Concept	Fitness	Investing
Avoiding FOMO	Sticking to a planned process of running, strength training or yoga will bring you some discomfort in the short run, but tremendous results in the long run. This involves shunning the hottest new workout plan in the short run.	Sticking to a disciplined investing process, whether it is buying funds through SIP route, or buying stocks at only reasonable valuations. One day, today's monthly salary will equal the SIP amount if we give it enough time.
Embracing boredom	Learning to sustain through periods where you are seeing no tangible progress, but trusting the plan for the long term.	Learning to sustain through periods of absolutely no returns in the portfolio, but knowing why you bought a stock or fund and trusting the long-term plan.
Tracking	Checking your weight or body-fat progress daily is going to make you anxious, but seeing it every week or month is where you will understand whether you are on track.	Daily tracking of your portfolio is going to cause you anxiety, but seeing it every three months, or better yet, six months, is a better way to track your progress.

As James Smith, Nutrition and Fitness Coach, said, 'It is never about tomorrow's habit, but today's action.'[17]

Scientists classify our present living conditions as a delayed-return environment, wherein individuals may invest years of effort before experiencing desired outcomes. This shift likely began with the advent of agriculture roughly 10,000 years ago, as farmers began cultivating crops with an extended waiting period for harvest. However, it's only in the past few centuries that our daily lives have primarily revolved around decisions with delayed returns, such as those concerning career trajectories, retirement savings and vacation planning, among other scheduled commitments.

There is also part of the brain called the nucleus accumbens that dictates our brain's 'anticipation of a reward' or ability to delay gratification.

A fascinating study showed how physical activity improved the nucleus accumbens, which dictates long-term decision making, and how sticking to a process of being regular with exercise shapes our ability to make decisions.[18] The study focussed on how strengthening of the nucleus accumbens ensured that no 'impulsive choices' were made and the ability to see into the horizon was not impaired.

Warren Buffett, although not the most ideal person to go to for health advice, made a very valid point of building habits early to develop the ability to delay gratification.[19] 'You get one only one body and one mind. And it's got to last a lifetime. Now, it's very easy to let them ride for many years. But if you don't take care of that mind and that body, they'll be a train-wreck forty years later. It's what you do right now, today, that determines how your mind and body will operate ten, twenty and thirty years from now.'

As neuroscientist Daniel Friedman puts it, 'The world is sensory rich and causal poor.'[20]

This means that treat will taste good in the moment, but we are less aware that eating the treat every day for months slowly leads to the accumulation of fat on our bodies.

Key Principles Learned from This Chapter

- The fruits of improving health and creating wealth follow the same principle of going through some form of pain in the short term to achieve something worthwhile in the distant future.
- Sacrificing something today does not necessarily mean we are losing out on today; in fact we are building a better tomorrow.
- All valuable things in life come at the expense of some form of sacrifice; there are no free lunches in life.

11

Ancient Wisdom

'I very frequently get the question, 'what's going to change in the next ten years?' That's a very interesting question. I almost never get the question, 'what's not going to change in the next ten years?' And I submit to you that that second question is actually the more important of the two.'

Jeff Bezos[1]

Let us now tell you the story of Mihir's grandparents, Shanta and Narayan. They began the day at six every morning with a brisk walk, followed by a cup of tea. They would normally have a filling breakfast, knowing that the next meal wouldn't come for a few hours. They would pack their lunchboxes and head to work—Narayan was a lawyer in a government job and Shanta was a librarian.

They lived on the fourth floor of a building which had no elevator. Narayan had to carry a heavy briefcase, while Shanta also carried some belongings. Shanta then headed to the bus stop, while Narayan made his way to the railway station. Shanta's commute was easier, with the bus dropping her off right at her workplace, while Narayan faced a more laborious journey: walking to the station, navigating a couple of bridges, boarding a train, disembarking, climbing another bridge, and finally walking to his office.

At lunch, both would relish their homemade food—chapatis, sabji, rice, dal, salad and an occasional fruit. That was the only meal they ate besides a cup of evening tea available at the tea stall below the office, a mandatory ritual with colleagues.

The commute repeated in the evening: Shanta on the bus, Narayan with the bridges, the train and the walks. At the end of it, both trekked up four floors to their home. And it was necessary to reach home by seven, not only to catch the news, but also to prepare dinner—another simple home-cooked meal. Sleep would be at a fixed time, before the cycle would repeat at 6 a.m. Life was not rushed and nothing was forced to fit the routine.

In today's day and age, we speak about this phenomenon more scientifically, using the term 'circadian rhythm' to refer to the body's natural twenty-four-hour sleep–wake cycle. However, our grandparents used to follow this as a daily practice without complicating their world with too many scientific terms.

Calories were in check due to a lack of easy availability, and any excess calories were burnt due to movement that was mandatory for them and not having everything available to them at the click of a button thanks to technology. They probably did not even know what calories meant, and probably did not even need to spend much time knowing the concept, as their food was always in check, and their movement was abundant.

But now, let's look at how Mihir's daily routine pans out. His day starts at 7.30 with a coffee to bring the body to its senses. Breakfast is skipped on most days because of his perpetual rush. He barely gets ready in time, books an Uber, and goes to the ground floor in an elevator one minute before it is about to reach. He has to meticulously plan his calorie count for the day because movement is not a luxury he can afford most of the day due to the sedentary nature of his work, but he acknowledges that and plans his day accordingly. He has to stay away from his food delivery apps because cravings for delicious food are something that he can fulfil with the click of a button, and regret later. He may or may not be able to sleep every day and follow a consistent routine of sleep due to the rushed nature of the day.

While Narayan's life was hard in a certain way, Mihir's life has become as hard because of the very technology that the former lacked. This is something that the modern world often fails to acknowledge.

Yuval Noah Harari covered this rapid change in his book *Sapiens*.[2] 'In the year 1500, there were about 500 million Homo Sapiens in the entire world. Today, there are seven billion. The total value of goods and services produced by humankind in the year 1500 is estimated at $250 billion, in today's dollars. Nowadays, the value of a year of human production is close to $60 trillion. In 1500, humanity consumed about 13 trillion calories of energy per day. Today, we consume 1,500 trillion calories a day. Take a second look at those figures—human population has increased fourteen-fold, production 240-fold, and energy consumption 115-fold.'

Luxuries tend to become necessities and spawn new obligations.

With the advent of rapid industrialization came the rapid rise in junk-food manufacturing too.[3] The basic logic behind this is that 'junk food makes us want to eat more'. Highly processed and calorie-dense foods often lack sufficient nutrients and fibre, leading to less satiety and a desire to consume more to feel satisfied.

On the other hand, nutritious food is designed to make us eat less. Whole, nutrient-dense foods like fruits, vegetables and lean proteins contain fibre, vitamins and minerals that promote feelings of fullness and satisfaction, naturally regulating appetite and reducing the urge to overeat.

Our ancestors never had access to artificially processed food; hence, they had the luxury of being able to stop eating beyond a certain point. Turn back to any of your old family albums, and you will mostly observe lean individuals from back in the day.

In the book *Made in India* by Milind Soman's mother, eighty-four years old and super fit, said that the generation that came after her was freed from physical labour and that is the reason that they *need to exercise*.

Their generation had no restaurants, no processed foods, nothing available at the click of a button.

Most things in life required movement.

Dr Peter Attia explains a key change happening today due to the access to processed food in his book *Outlive*.[4] Many novel diseases present today were practically non-existent back in the day. Type 2 diabetes emerged in the early-1700s, and was at first largely a disease of the super-elite, such as popes, artists, wealthy merchants and nobles who could afford this newly fashionable luxury food known as sugar.

By the early twentieth century, diabetes was becoming a disease of the masses and was growing at a rapid pace, with the easy availability of sugar and other processed foods which harm the population.

Attia states that our metabolism has evolved over millennia, and it is not equipped to deal with the ultramodern diet that has appeared over the last century or so. Evolution adapted our body in such a way that we need to eat to store fat to endure periods of time without food, and therefore, this stored energy would come in use. Hence, our ancestors were able to endure periods of difficult times with this stored energy. However, these genes passed on in a negative way, so that now, our body asks to store nutrients as fat, but as soon as we feel the slightest level of hunger, we have easy access to unlimited calories at the click of a button.

'Bodies that evolved to move all day sit slack and limp on comfy chairs and sofas, absorbing the world through bright screens like French fries under a heat lamp,' said evolutionary anthropologist Herman Pontzer, and it perfectly captures how the world has become a less healthy place from Narayan's days to Mihir's.[5]

Food historian Manoshi Bhattacharya mentions that physician Robert Tattersall says in his book *Diabetes: The Biography*, 'Much of the evidence that diabetes was a disease of the rich comes from India. The Indian experience suggested that mental work and excessive consumption of starches and sugars, aggravated by a completely sedentary life were to blame. This was certainly true of the "Bengali Babu" (a clerk who could write English), whose girth had a great tendency to increase in direct proportion to any increment to his pay.'[6]

However, Bhattacharya points out that local physician C.L. Bose wrote in 1907, 'Diabetes is almost unknown among Hindu widows, who lead a most unexciting life, and are not indulged in excess of saccharine or other farinaceous foods.'

Ancient Wisdom

Sadashiv, my (Ankush's) grandfather, worked as an income tax officer and was the sole bread-earner for his family. His mantra was simple—work hard at his job and put a little bit of money that he didn't need into financial instruments that could allow him to peacefully build a retirement corpus.

He had limited options, so most money would be put in fixed deposits due to the attractive rates. The little bit left over was put into the market, and these holdings were to be for the very long term.

Every month, Sadashiv's adviser would come to his home to collect a cheque for a recurring fixed deposit, small parts in quality blue-chip companies, and a very small portion in a mutual fund.

This was the only way his generation knew for a salaried person to build a respectable life; to ensure that he has enough corpus to live out his days and pass something on to the next generation. There was no information overload, and a simple concept of achieving financial freedom—by saving monthly and investing into simple financial products.

Today, I (Ankush) enjoy easy access to a wealth of information and believe I can outdo what my grandfather and previous generations could not achieve due to their lack of access to such information. I open my Twitter app and encounter a 1000x multibagger stock that could potentially change my life. After doing my own research and coupled with the conviction the expert has in the stock, I invest, but within a short span of time, I find myself sitting on a huge loss while this expert moves on to the next 1000x idea to share with his followers.

Every day, I see a tweet that shatters the pre-existing notions of what I need to do to make money, when the simple answer was to follow what my grandfather did. I look back to his days and start the process of putting money every month in an SIP, and within five years, I am more content and certain about what I need to do to obtain some form of financial freedom.

The instruments might not be the same as Sadashiv used, but the process Ankush follows is inspired by his grandfather—learning to think long term.

As James Clear said, 'Today's habits are modern-day solutions to ancient desires. New versions of old vices. The underlying motives of human behaviour remain the same.'[7]

~

Chanakya was an ancient Indian philosopher, economist, and political strategist who played a key role in the establishment of the Maurya Empire. He warned against wealth acquired dishonestly, a principle relevant even today as financial fraud and corruption persist.[8] The collapse of large companies due to unethical practices stands testament to his teachings.

Conversely, the reason why the mutual fund industry continues to grow steadily is because of regulatory transparency and ethics. It is one of the few industries where Chanakya's teaching to grow wealth in a sustainable manner can be applied.

Chanakya's writings, particularly in his famous work *Arthashastra*, do emphasize the importance of wealth management, including investments in various assets such as gold. This tradition of including gold in one's asset allocation has carried on till this day in Indian traditions, and is now even available through digital instruments.

Devdutt Pattanaik, in his book *12 Ways to Get Rich*, describes how the power of compounding in investing has been mentioned far back in Indian mythology.[9] As per the Bhagavad Gita, we look at our income as fruit ('phala') and seed ('beeja').

Fruit is the money used to pay our bills, repay debt and buy property.

Seed is the money used to invest in assets which can grow fruit for the future.

We can help others by lending money or investing in their business. The former is a form of debt investing where the investment is made to purely bear fruit, and the latter is a form of equity investing where the investment is considered as planting a seed, which will eventually grow into a tree. Just as a seed takes a long time to bear fruit, investments take a long time to generate returns.

Another story from Indian mythology that's relevant to this subject is that of the three yoginis, Vimala, Nirmala, and Kamala, which explained how patience was the key trait in investing.

The first yogini, Vimala, ate a golden fruit and swallowed its golden seed. The next day, she was hungry again, and went looking for another fruit.

The second, Nirmala, ate a golden fruit and planted the seed. She waited for the plant to grow to bear the golden fruit. But she got impatient when the tree did not grow to bear fruit. She cut the tree and gave its golden wood to a carpenter in exchange for a large quantity of regular fruit that satisfied her hunger, but only for a year.

The third yogini, Kamala, ate the golden fruit, planted the golden seed, and waited patiently for the tree to grow and bear the golden fruit. The tree bore a hundred golden fruits, and thus, Kamala learnt the value of patience. She went on planting seeds, and fifty of those trees bore fifty fruits each, thereby leading to 2,500 fruits for Kamala. She was even able to take care of Vimala and Nirmala and teach them the tricks of the trade.

In a study on what kept the ancient Greeks so lean, researchers studied how back in the fifth and fourth centuries

BCE, citizens detested the effects of ageing and considered it an incurable disease.[10]

Things changed between the first century BCE and the first century CE when Cicero and others began to view ageing as a modifiable condition. In his *'Essay on Old Age'*, written in 44 BCE, Roman philosopher Cicero mentioned, 'It is our duty to resist old age, to compensate for its defects, to fight against it as we would fight a disease; to adopt a regimen of health; to practice moderate exercise; and to take just enough food and drink to restore our strength.'

The Romans' ancient tradition of strength training showed the world the importance of practice.

The ancient religion and culture of Jainism inculcates the habit of fasting for many hours to cleanse the body; it is also considered a way to cleanse the soul. Islam also has a strong culture of fasting during Ramzan, which is a practice used for purification of the body, passed on from tradition.

These ancient cultures inculcated intermittent fasting long before it was a marketing tool for weight loss.

The Jewish tradition is to teach people from the get-go about not being envious of others, and it is a discipline ingrained in most people who follow these teachings.

Indian communities such as Marwaris and Gujaratis are known to be the wealthiest not only because of their acumen for business, but also because of their traditions of being frugal in business.

While we have learnt from our ancestors about the principles of health and wealth, it is important that we also become aware of what happens to the generations that succeed us. This can be well understood by Pottenger's cat experiment, which showed that a diet of processed food affects the health of every subsequent generation, and we are lucky to have not inherited this from our previous generations.[11]

Francis Pottenger, a physician, proved this theory through a ten-year, multiple-generation experiment involving 900 cats. He began the study by removing the adrenal glands of the cats and dividing them into two groups.[12] One group was served fresh meat and raw milk, while the other was fed processed milk and meat. The cats that were fed fresh, unprocessed food recovered significantly faster.

Pottenger conducted more experiments in controlled environments, but the same result kept repeating: the group with fresh food recovered significantly faster.

The first generation of cats that ate fresh food developed 20 per cent fewer skeletal problems or crooked teeth, and had more calcium in their bones. In contrast, the first generation of the second group had weak jawbones and teeth, and much less calcium in their bones.

The condition of the second group's third and fourth generations kept deteriorating. In contrast, there was no change in the health status of the first group's subsequent generations. In fact, each generation turned out slightly healthier than the one before it.

This demonstrates that DNA is more of a blueprint than a commandment, and being mindful early on can have a positive impact on our next generation. We are fortunate to have had ancestors with minimal access to processed foods.

On the wealth front too, taking on debt to fuel our dreams can negatively impact the well-being of our next generation. We can observe many debt-fuelled nations today suffering the consequences of what their predecessors took for granted.

Urdu texts from the last millennium teach us this concept through the jaagir and amaanat systems.[13] Amaanat implies trusteeship—we don't own it, but are a temporary custodian tasked with passing it on safely to future generations. Jaagir, on the other hand, implies ownership—we have absolute rights with no expectations of prudence.

Many Western countries have been burdened by debt from previous generations, who were thinking of their own times. Now, current generations are reeling under what has been passed on to them. Had they turned to the concepts of amaanat and jaagir, they could have been in a better place.

Bad loans are common—companies or individuals take on debt to fuel growth or live a certain lifestyle. The scars of the burns caused by these bad loans are passed on to future generations.

In Indian mythology, 'greed' is being consumed by our own hunger at the cost of those who feed us. When we're in need, we seek swarga (heaven) for ourselves and others. When we're greedy, we seek swarga for ourselves, even if it means pushing others into naraka (hell).

This comes down to differentiating between need and greed, as explained by Devdutt Pattanaik in *12 Ways to Get Rich*, where he says that 'need' is seeking to satisfy our hunger and the hunger of those who feed us.

When we start treating our wealth as a jaagir, the next generation suffers. Holding true to an amaanat system allows us to enjoy our lives in the moment, while also safely passing on custody to our next generation.

We should be thankful to our ancestors for not having passed down the genetics of poor health or the baggage of poor financial decisions. We, in turn, can be better humans by not passing on either to our future generations.

To develop foresight, one has to have an idea of hindsight, and this can also be learnt from ancient traditions. Unlike previous generations, we have access to various other traditions to learn from.

In *Sapiens*, Yuval Noah Harari explains the 'gorging gene' theory.[14] Our primal instincts as hunter–gatherers persist within us, influencing our behaviour even in modern times. The abundance of high-calorie foods readily available today mirrors the scarcity our ancestors faced, driving a subconscious urge to indulge. This evolutionary trait contributes significantly to the global epidemic of obesity.

In ancient environments, sugary treats were rare finds amid sparse resources. Imagine a forager from 30,000 years ago encountering a fig tree—the logical response would be to consume as many figs as possible before they were devoured by other creatures. This innate drive to consume calorie-dense foods became ingrained in our genetic makeup.

This disconnect between our environment and our DNA explains why we might devour an entire tub of ice cream accompanied by a large soda when presented with the opportunity, as if we were still navigating the savannahs of our ancestors.

Today, we live in a calorie-rich environment, but our brain continues to crave food like it is scarce.

When our ancestors used to eat natural carb-heavy foods at meal times, there was a high probability that they went out to do physical work with the energy accumulated through the food, or they simply ate it to replenish energy from all the movement they had done through the day.

In our day and age, we are literally going back to sit at our office desk most of the time.

We have just carried over the same tradition to the corporate world, with no understanding of how the food was being utilized by our ancestors.

There is no coincidence that obesity and many other diseases have been rampantly increasing over this century.

The first popular 'diet' was officially introduced in the English language in 1864 through William Banting's own experience. He documented it in a pamphlet titled, 'Letter on corpulence addressed to the public'.[15] In fact, before it was called a 'diet', it was recommended for people to 'Bant'.

Banting's was the first document recommending a high-protein, low-carb plan. His meals largely incorporated high amounts of protein over three meals, with dashes of fruit and toast at times. He lost thirty-five pounds over that period despite a considerable allowance of alcohol in his regimen.

As he described it, 'I have not felt better now than in my last twenty-six years, my other body ailments have become matters of history.'

The wise have always emphasized on the same simple principles across centuries; fools have tried to be different in every generation, and have failed.

Key Principles Learned from This Chapter

- The ancient principles of health and wealth never die, they just present themselves in different avatars from one generation to the next.
- History and tradition have a lot to teach us about health and wealth if we spend enough time studying them.

12

Healthy Is Wealthy

Almost any ambitious person will say, 'I want to focus on wealth creation in the beginning of my career, after which I can take care of my health.'

The prevalent perception in the modern world is that once we start pursuing wealth, there must be a like-for-like trade-off with our health, because we lack the time for it. This harmful myth has led people to believe it's acceptable to neglect their health using ambition as an excuse.

Unfortunately, it becomes harder for us with each passing day to prioritize our health, as we looked at in the habit-formation example in the chapter on delayed gratification.

As individuals ascend the corporate hierarchy, increased disposable income results in more unhealthy choices, given the extensive array of options available to them.

It might be assumed that a wealthier individual would have sufficient knowledge about the concept of healthy eating and, at the very least, possess the means to make healthier food choices compared to a lower-income consumer who has limited options and is likely to lack knowledge due to resource constraints.

However, data from India's National Family Health Survey (NFHS) tells a different story.[1] A detailed study of the numbers for the period 2019 to 2021, conducted by *ThePrint*, brought attention to a troubling pattern: the rise in obesity within households with higher disposable incomes.[2] The wealth categories were segmented into five quintiles, spanning from the lowest 20 per cent of the population at the base of the wealth pyramid to the top 20 per cent of the wealth distribution. The period witnessed a 12.6 per cent obesity rate among women (one in eight) in India's highest wealth group.

In stark contrast, the obesity rate in the lowest 20 per cent of the wealth group stood at a mere 1.6 per cent of women aged 15–49. For men, the obesity rate was 8 per cent in the top wealth quintile and only 1.2 per cent in the bottom quintile.

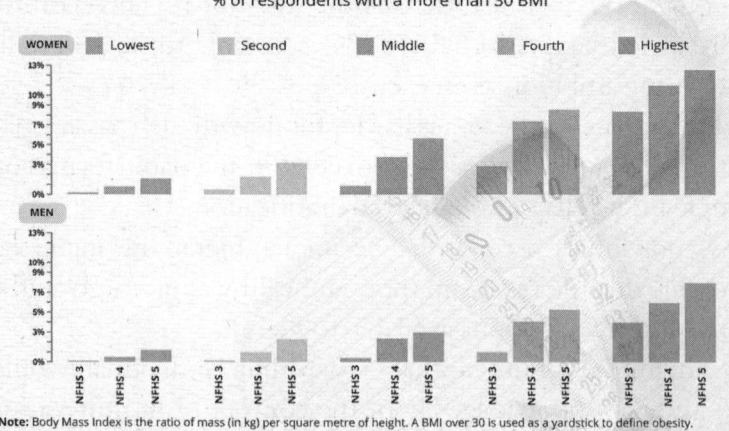

Source: ThePrint, February 2023

The obesity percentage for women was higher because their metabolic rate is lower than that of men, meaning they gain weight more quickly when consuming the same number of calories.

The analysis has been conducted across multiple cycles of the NFHS, so it is not biased to a specific time period. 'For instance, in 2005–06, for every 100 women in the middle-income group, there wasn't even one woman who was found to be obese (0.9 per cent). Fast forward to 2019–21, and nearly one in every seventeen women in the middle wealth quintile is obese (5.7 per cent). The obesity rate among wealthier women in the top quintile has jumped from 8.4 per cent (one in twelve) to 12.6 per cent (one in eight),' the report states.

'The rate of obesity among men is relatively low, but the trend is similar. Only 0.4 per cent of men in the middle wealth quintile were reported to be obese in 2005–06, but this rose to 3 per cent in 2019–21,' it adds.

This clearly shows how more disposable income gives rise to more consumption, and not necessarily healthier consumption.

In the United States, as per a study done by the USD Economic Research Service between 1970 and 2014, as per capita income increased, the foods consumed from outside the home has increased from 26 per cent in 1970 to 50.1 per cent in 2014. The United States has one of the highest obesity rates in the world.[3]

A 2013 study showed that excess calorie consumption could lead to cancer, as it is formed by an abundance of energy in the cells. Types of cancer that can be caused by obesity include endometrial, oesophageal adenocarcinoma, colorectal, postmenopausal breast, prostate and renal.

This goes to show why today, 'wealth belly' has become an increasingly common term, and although it is seemingly used jokingly by people, we believe it's a way to mask insecurity. We asked WebGPT to define the term, and it responded: 'Wealth belly refers to a softly rounded body type associated with a life of luxury, including indulgence in good food and wine, signifying great wealth. It represents a lifestyle marked by abundance and indulgence.'

That last line highlights a key point—that abundance can be a double-edged sword and leads to indulgence.

We spoke about dopamine and abundance early on in the book, and this abundance can often have a damaging impact on the lives of individuals. It becomes difficult to reverse a lifestyle of abundance once it becomes ingrained. That belly eventually leads to a whole host of metabolic diseases.

It is not rocket science to understand that a healthier person automatically becomes more productive at the workplace, thereby leading to increased profitability for a company.

When we think of exercise, we tend to only look at the physical benefits, but science has proven time and again how exercise has powerful brain-changing effects and impacts the way we think and feel. It provides:

1. Improved concentration
2. Sharper memory
3. Faster learning
4. Prolonged mental stamina
5. Enhanced creativity
6. Lower stress

Instead of viewing exercise as something we do for ourselves, it's time we started considering physical activity as part of 'work' itself. We're not abandoning work. On the contrary, we're ensuring that the hours we've put in have value.

Exercising also helps the body release endorphins—'happy hormones'—thereby elevating our mood, which has positive effects on workplace performance. All of our jobs require us to build relationships and collaborate to foster growth. Within this context, feeling irritable is no longer simply an inconvenience—no one wants to get to work on a Monday morning and meet an irritable colleague. If you don't want to meet them, aim to make yourself that non-irritable colleague.

Being fit makes for less sick days lost, more staff at peak performance—factors which eventually lead to a more productive workforce, which should logically lead to more profitability for companies.

There is no perfect time for anyone to schedule a workout; some prefer five in the morning while some like ten o'clock at night. The point is that we should allocate some time in our schedule for a workout.

If you are a professional investor or someone who is passionate about investing, you would have used the word 'capital allocation' a lot. If you are well-versed with this term, you would know that allocation of capital to the investee company's most productive assets, more often than not, produces the best returns.

That capital allocation definition extends beyond just investing and to most facets of life.

We can use this same analogy to understand that allocating a certain amount of time for exercise would produce a benefit for our body.

To those who think that exercising makes one feel tired at work, and use it as an excuse to skip it altogether, we want to point out that maybe you are doing it wrong, because the whole point of exercise is to make you feel more energetic throughout the day.

Health has no defined monetary value or linear status in society. It's a single-player game. We won't be able to tangibly measure the value of good health in society, unlike money or status. At the end of the day, our work must define our worth, and this is a fair fact.

However, the greatest irony lies in the fact that our long-term success at work will be determined by our mental and physical levels of cognition, and this is driven by a focus on one's health.

While there may not be immediate monetary benefits, it indirectly contributes in some way to the quality of the work, which people often fail to acknowledge.

If we aim to endure those fourteen- to sixteen-hour workdays, we need to be physically and mentally fit to do so. We firmly believe that even small habits such as walking more and being mindful of our diet can make a significant difference in the quality of those hours at work.

Isn't it beginning to look ironic that we think putting in long hours means sacrificing the time we would need for health? In reality, a healthier person will be able to sustain those hours for a much longer period. Someone who maintains a healthy lifestyle will have the energy to attend more meetings and the mental capacity to stay focussed on a screen for extended hours while effectively handling more tasks. This is simply common sense.

Charles Darwin wrote, 'In the struggle for survival, the fittest win out at the expense of their rivals because they succeed in adapting themselves best to their environment.'[5]

Survival of the fittest is not about being the strongest or the fastest; as Darwin stated, the 'fittest' actually means those who are flexible and can make adjustments to match their environment and circumstances. Those are the skills that make us survivors.

To add on to Darwin's point, those who adapt themselves to be physically fit enough to meet their schedules will most likely be mentally fit enough to meet their schedule as well.

This pictorial from James Clear highlights how the inputs in our body dictate the output we are able to produce.[6]

Source: JamesClear.com

Training is a derivative of decent sleep and eating habits. Training regularly, eating well and sleeping well makes us more productive at work or school.

The CEOs of the largest Indian corporations have been flag-bearers of sticking to healthy exercise routines. Harish Mariwala, chairman of Marico, said in an article, 'Pandemic or no pandemic, I exercise every day.'[7, 8]

Bob Iger, the CEO of Disney, has a disciplined minute-to-minute schedule, which begins with exercise. The likes of Apple CEO Tim Cook, Meta boss Mark Zuckerberg and Virgin Group founder Richard Branson have also been flag-bearers highlighting the importance of making time for exercise in their schedules. On the domestic front, Zerodha's Nithin Kamath has been a huge proponent of health and regularly speaks about it on public platforms.[9, 10]

Nimesh Mehta, MD and CEO of one of India's largest asset and wealth management companies, blows the mind of readers of his book *Sales Booster* with the story of how his transformation shaped his personal and career growth, despite being bound by time and an accident that could have physically paralysed him.[11] He has been highly successful in leading companies and highlights the importance of a plan.

Source: *Sales Booster* by Nimesh Mehta.

One could argue that certain individuals can afford to focus on health because they have wealth, but that statement is only partially true. Working in a corporate environment makes us aware of the kind of impact that work stress has on health, and even more so with leaders who are accountable for a large part of important company decisions.

Apart from individuals, let's see what certain organizations have done to incentivize a healthier work culture (subject to updates by these companies):

Wellness company Casper introduced bonus incentives for employees achieving stated fitness goals.[12] Google is renowned for its dedication to the well-being of its employees; it not only offers on-site fitness centres, but also provides more than 200 exercise classes, including eclectic options like 'how to dance at a party'.[13] International Business Machines' (IBM's) old HR manual for employees gives interesting insights too—apart from insurance and healthcare benefits, the company earmarked 'Nutrition Tuesdays' and 'Workout Wednesdays' to discuss these topics with employees.[14]

Mark Bertolini, CEO of US insurance giant Aetna, stated how promoting exercise programmes for employees led to a reduction in wellness costs by almost 7 per cent and helped increase productivity of employees, thereby leading to increased profitability for the company.[15]

Now let's look at some interesting data points on opportunity costs that industries face if their employees lack focus on their health.

Back pain among employees is a common occurrence, and according to research conducted in 2006, the total costs of low-back pain in the US exceeded $100 billion per year.[16] The cost of treatment itself accounted for $30 billion of these, while the issues caused loss of productivity worth $30–40 billion, and a similar amount was lost in terms of wages. Nearly two decades later, these numbers can be expected to be much higher. These people could've all been helped by strengthening their lower backs, while focussing on nutrition could've reduced chronic inflammation in the back muscles, another study showed.[17]

Sleep becomes tricky for those who may not have time, based on their professions, even if they try their best. Nevertheless, sleep is important and can ultimately impact global economies, because it helps with improved memory, stronger immune systems, higher energy levels and better moods.

Studies highlight that the prevalence of short sleep (less than six hours per night) among American adults has increased over the past decades. By 2017, around 32.9 per cent of adults reported getting less than six hours of sleep nightly, reflecting a rise from 28.6 per cent in 2004.[18] The sleep deprivation epidemic has been slowly catching up to us, and we can expect this to get worse going forward.

Data released in 2015 by the global policy think-tank RAND Corporation on sleep loss and GDP showed that the US sustains by far the highest economic losses (up to $411 billion a year, which is 2.28 per cent of its GDP) due to the size of its economy, followed by Japan (up to $138 billion a year, which is 2.92 per cent of its GDP). Germany (up to $60 billion, 1.56 per cent of its GDP) and the UK (up to $50 billion, 1.86 per cent of its GDP) have similar losses.[19] Among developed countries, Canada has the lowest financial losses due to lack of sleep (up to $21.4 billion, which is 1.35 per cent of its GDP).[20]

Small changes in sleep duration could have a big impact on the economy—for example, if individuals who slept under six hours started sleeping six to seven hours, this could add $226.4 billion to the US economy, $75.7 billion to the Japanese economy, $34.1 billion to the German economy, $29.9 billion to the UK economy and $12 billion to the Canadian economy.

Healthy Is Wealthy

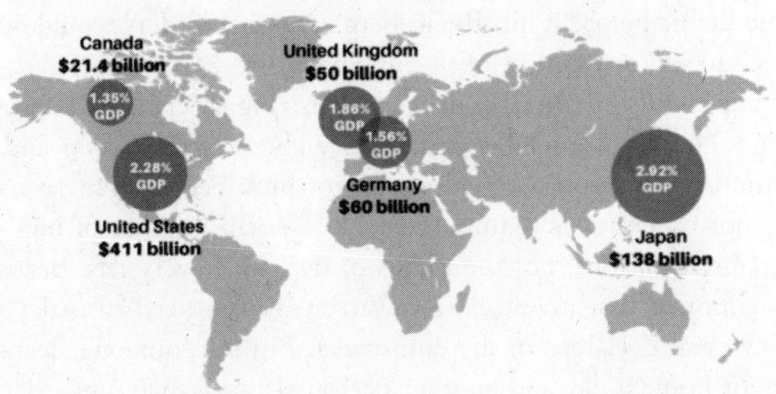

Source: Rand Corporation 2015 data.

The McKinsey Institute also showed in a 2021 study that the sleep-loss epidemic is affecting the global economy.[21]

'Sleep-related absence from work is thought to account for the loss of ten million working hours a year in the United States, 4.8 million in Japan, and 1.7 million in Germany. Lost sleep also takes a toll on productivity: an analysis using data from US companies puts the annual cost at $1,300 to $3,000 per employee,' it stated.

On a lighter note, investment managers are always on the hunt for companies that are compounding their earnings; so, why not add the sleep patterns of employees and promoters as a filter when screening for companies based on the above statistics?

In a famous TED Talk, Ariana Huffington, founder of the *Huffington Post* (now *HuffPost*), said the way to a more productive and joyful life is getting enough sleep.[22] She told an interesting story about the time she went out for dinner with a man who bragged about how he got only four hours of sleep to put in more hours at work, and says she wanted to tell him he would be a more interesting person if he got five hours of sleep, but controlled herself. She said being a good leader is like 'steering the titanic before it hits the iceberg', and that leaders would do well to set the example of sleeping better.

Speaking of good leaders emphasizing sleep, Jeff Bezos, in a great talk, said he prioritizes eight hours of sleep and, among other things, it helps him to think better.[23] He says a senior executive is required to make a small number of high-quality decisions, not thousands of decisions every day. Bezos mentioned that investors like Warren Buffett need to make a few great decisions in the entire year. But say someone sleeps eight hours a day and another person sleeps four hours a day. On paper it looks like the second person has four more hours of productivity in the day. Assuming that the person who slept eight hours has around twelve hours of productive time during the day, on paper the person who slept for four hours has sixteen hours of productive time in the same day.[24] That equates to around 33 per cent more time to make decisions. As a result, instead of 100 decisions, the person can make 133 decisions. But what's the point of those decisions if their quality comes down due to lack of sleep?

Outside of obvious costs, like salaries and benefits, there are invisible costs that employers miss out on. Staff well-being can have a profound impact on finances of companies too.

1. 'Presenteeism', defined as coming to work while sick, cost American businesses over $150 billion in 2022.[25]
2. Working while sick costs the economy $173 billion.
3. Poor health can mean higher insurance premiums and more sick days.
4. Heart failure comes at a cost of $220 billion.[26]

A Harvard Health study suggests that a twenty-year-old who goes from being 'obese' down to 'overweight' would save an average of $17,655 in direct medical costs and productivity losses over their lifetime.[27] If the same person were to go from being obese to a healthy weight, the average savings would go up to $28,020. A forty-year-old who goes from being obese to overweight can save an average of $18,262, and if the same person goes down to a healthy weight, the average savings could be $31,447.

There isn't enough data available on this particular subject on the Indian subcontinent, so we have used data from the United States to highlight opportunity costs. However, it is safe to assume each country bears the brunt of these invisible costs in its own way.

In the book *Richer, Wiser, Happier* by William Green, I (Ankush) came across multiple prominent fund managers and individual investors, but the most intriguing is Ken Shubin Stein from Stein Capital Management.[28] Before becoming a hedge-fund manager and teaching the advanced investment research course at Columbia Business School, he spent two decades as a fund manager at Stein Capital Management, his holding company, which had 400 employees. But he is also steeped in science, having conducted research in molecular genetics, trained as a surgeon, and founded the International Concussion Society.

It's particularly fascinating that in the service of his professional work, Stein makes a concerted effort to improve his health and wellness to hone his investment-management skills.

'There are four things that we know improve brain health and function—meditation, exercise, sleep and nutrition,' Stein says in the book.

Determined to use every tool at his disposal, he exercised strenuously, which also helped him to sleep better. He ate more fish, vegetables and fruit, and renounced his 'worst tendencies, including a habit of handling stress by gorging on vanilla ice cream with mashed up chocolate chip cookies'. He also developed a regular meditation practice, which he calls 'a mission-critical habit for many successful investors'.

Stein goes on to talk about how these habits have a compounding effect over the longer term.

'The reason you meditate is not because it is important on a specific day; regular practice will help you handle the hard setbacks and will keep you constantly prepared for them. Having that practice in place prepares you well. It's a lot like preventive medicine,' he says.

Stein also attaches tremendous importance to cognitive biases, and underlines the need to guard against them. Cognitive biases are connected with mental and emotional health, and are often caused and influenced by negative emotional states. Mental and emotional health, in turn, have a symbiotic relationship with physical health. And they are all extremely important, not merely for our overall well-being, but also for effective work performance.

Stein uses an acronym, HALT-PS (hunger, anger, loneliness, tiredness, pain and stress), as a reminder to pause when certain factors might be impairing his judgement, and postpones important decisions until his brain is in a position to function better.

Green's book also refers to a paper published by the *Annual Review of Psychology* in 2015, which found that 'emotions, powerfully, predictably and pervasively influence decision making'.[29] The research focussed on how sadness increased tendencies to favour high-risk, high-reward options, while anxiety increased tendencies to favour low-risk, low-reward options.

An important lesson Green draws from Stein's account is that we need to be self-aware and honest with ourselves in order to understand when our emotional state is likely to compromise our judgement and performance. This is a vital guiding principle, be it in investing or in life.

Stein used his HALT-PS framework in the 2020 Covid period to ensure that his 'internal state' was not compromised while treating patients. He drew on all his learnings like eating well, moving as much as possible, and said even 'slow breathing for ten seconds in the bathroom before entering the ICU to treat a patient' made a world of a difference.

So, instead of viewing exercise as something we do for ourselves, it's time we started considering physical activity as part of the work itself. We're not abandoning work; on the contrary, we're ensuring that the hours we put in have more value.

A *Harvard Business Review* study by Jim Loehr and Tony Schwartz, titled 'The making of a corporate athlete', highlighted that if athletes with career spans of ten to fifteen years can put in so much effort to take care of their lifestyle in order to ensure they are giving their best, individuals in the corporate world, where the career span is at least thirty years, can take some inspiration to ensure peak/optimum performance.[30]

The research focussed on how leaders from various fields were able to focus on making changes in their spiritual, emotional, mental and physical capacities, and this translated to better performance at work and the ability to adapt to a high-stress environment without feeling a loss of energy and cognition.

When we are stressed, we want quick answers and decisions. It makes us take poor decisions in the moment. In fact, there is a science to that too. Healthier individuals typically have a lower resting heart rate and have lesser activation of their sympathetic nervous system—the part of our body that gets activated during moments of stress. Folks who work out more and have healthier nervous systems have a relatively lesser activation of this part, thereby leading to better decision making.

Under stress, the body raises the level of cortisol (the stress hormone), thereby impairing our decision-making abilities.

The longer we live and the better our quality of life, the more number of years we have to build and, most importantly, enjoy our wealth.

Can you visit ten stores across various parts of the city to sell products, then come home and reply to two dozen emails and answer ten phone calls? Can you sit for hours in front a screen if your cognitive mind is not allowing you to? Can you do this all and still have time with your family and to play with your kids? If you end each day massively exhausted, how is your body going to wake up consistently for many years to do the same routine over and over?

'I don't have time' is usually an 'it's not my priority' problem. The things we prioritize always fall into place regardless of how 'busy' we are. Life adjusts itself to our priorities.

Key Principles Learned from This Chapter

- It's a myth that we need to sacrifice health for wealth. We use it as an excuse because we do not prioritize health enough.
- A lack of health leads to a lack of wealth, as shown by data on opportunity costs incurred by companies and economies.
- Healthy is the new wealthy.

Acknowledgements

Ankush's Note

A large part of this book came from standing on the shoulders of giants, and imitating great people who have followed these principles through their lives in their own ways. The book is a consolidation of all these learnings coupled with personal experiences into the principles of health and wealth.

This book would not have been possible without writers and practitioners who documented their in-depth research to inspire my style of writing and thinking. I pay complete homage to these people for many of the inspirations in this book, and also for shaping me as a person, which allowed me to live life in a way that allowed me to write this book. I just applied the learnings that these teachers had to share with the world, and though we have never met, I am their ardent student.

It is rightly said the kind of books we read shape us as people, as well as our way of thinking, and I would like to thank all those I have quoted here and been inspired by:

- *Dopamine Nation* by Anna Lembke
- *Good to Great* by Jim Collins

- *What I Learned About Investing from Darwin* by Pulak Prasad
- *Value Investing and Behavorial Finance* by Parag Parikh
- *Not A Diet Book* by James Smith
- *The Joys of Compounding* by Gautam Baid
- *Dollars and Sense* by Dan Ariely
- *The Body* by Bill Bryson
- *The Psychology of Money* by Morgan Housel
- *Atomic Habits* by James Clear
- *How the Mighty Fall* by Jim Collins
- *Your Money and Your Brain* by Jason Zweig
- *12 Ways to Get Rich* by Devdutt Pattanaik
- *Expectations Investing* by Michael Maboussin
- *Let's Talk Mutual Funds* by Monika Halan
- *Your Money Your Brain* by Jason Zweig
- *Sapiens* by Yuval Noah Harari
- *Outlived* by Peter Attia

There are a few other people who won't take credit for playing a part in my journey to writing a book, but I must pay tributes regardless.

My uncle Nitin Datar, who helped me in the process of editing and refining my writing when I had started blogging in 2019. Being a lawyer and astute reader, he was able to pick out every minute detail that needed to be refined in my blogs. I would submit a blog post to him on email and wait for days in anticipation for his edits so that I could consider and make the changes.

My friend Hisham Syed, who would be surprised to see his name here. He was the first one who thought my blogs were good enough, and nudged me to work as a freelance writer for a health-tech start-up in 2019, which led to a more formal writing practice outside of work over the weekends. This built the discipline of writing formally and also allowed me to prioritize time management over the weekends, a practice which greatly helped me write this book while managing the pressure of my full-time job.

Shashank Mehta, for deciding to read my blog on caffeine in 2020 and approaching me to contribute articles for the *Truth Be Told* newsletter.

My friend Samarth Bansal, from whom I learnt a lot about how to write for an audience. His detailed research, ruthless feedback and search for the truth inspired me to be a more responsible writer and understand the importance of being ruthless with editing. He will humbly not accept any applause for this, but he doesn't get to decide this time.

Shreya Punj, our consultant, who helped us make the idea of this book into reality. I mentioned her name before too, but it needs to be acknowledged again, because she is also someone who'll be too humble to take credit.

My dear friend Revati Banerji, who promptly helped me in creating illustrations of certain images in this book.

Sachin Sharma, our publisher, for being the most cooperative, motivating and supporting editor to work with. It has been a very comfortable journey working with him, and he has helped us with the editing and formatting of the book to suit the reader's perspective.

My boss at work, Nishit Shah, the manager of our fund, who gave me a ringside view of the investment-management process. Through my work experience, I have been able to navigate through cycles of the stock market while understanding how to manage clients' money and their psychology over the years. These real-life experience gave me more experience on the emotions of human beings than any theory I have read.

My late grandmother, whom I never met, but whose writing tales and stories let me live her life vicariously. My grandfather, who was an astute writer in his own right, but used to keep his journals for his own personal records. Luckily, I had access to them, and learnt the habit of journaling from him.

My parents, who allowed me to pursue my own career path, supported my decision to abruptly quit law after my graduation while studying for a professional exam, and allowed me to venture into the world of finance. I don't take this privilege—which few in the world may have—for granted. In fact, my father always harped on the importance of writing things you read, lest you forget them. I failed to take his advice too seriously in school, but it has helped me hone my process of writing. It's ironic how often your parents are just looking to give you advice for your betterment, but when you are young, you may be too naïve and arrogant to acknowledge it.

I started this wonderful journey of working out in 2011 with the intention to just look good. But I fell in love with it, and have learnt the importance of overall health. I would like to express sincere gratitude to all the trainers and nutritionists who shared their knowledge to empower me in becoming the healthiest version of myself. It is through this journey, mixed with my professional experience and reading, that I was able to connect the dots of the principles of health and wealth.

Writing is a lonely and personal journey that sometimes gets overwhelming, so I thank various authors like Ryan Holiday, Steven Pressfield, Ruskin Bond, Stephen King, David Perell, Rick Rubin, Amit Varma, and others who I may have missed out on, whose personal documentations on the process of writing always gave me inspiration to keep on going, and to navigate the feelings of 'impostor syndrome', anxiety and self-doubt.

Just as with investing, fitness and nutrition, writing demands a disciplined process. In fact, from the writing process, you can learn a lot about the power of compounding too!

Mihir's Note

We used the word 'serendipity' to describe how we met and this book was conceptualized. Now, it's time to thank the people whom we met serendipitously and who helped make the book what it is.

Shreya Punj, for giving us the confidence to write and helping us find a publisher. If not for Shreya, this book would not have happened.

Sachin Sharma, for being the most supportive, non-intrusive and yet effective publisher. We cannot thank him enough for helping us shape the content, flow, the timing of release and many other things.

Jitendra Chouksey, a.k.a. JC, for teaching me quantified nutrition; he continues to lead by example. My cousin Dr Amit Prabhu for being a shining example of extreme discipline and introducing me to JC. It was Amit who first advised me on how to get fit, and say goodbye to my cholesterol, fatty liver and hypertension permanently.

Thanks to our families for dissing our advice (as family is expected to do), but still supporting our endeavours. Ankush's dad for proving that it is never too early or too late to begin one's fitness journey. My parents, Urmila and Vivek Patki, for inculcating a sense of living below means for decades, because without this approach, my life would have not been as happy and content as it is today.

My wife Payal, for planning and executing quantified meals for years—especially meticulously planning my non-vegetarian food despite being a vegetarian herself.

Thanks also to my co-founders from Multipie—Sandeep Baid and Raj Singhal—for the life lessons before, during and after it. And to Krishna Iyer for being a mentor who has always been available.

Notes

Scan this QR code to access the detailed notes.

About the Authors

Ankush Datar is an investment professional, health and fitness enthusiast, and writer. He has been working in the professional investing field for the last eight years and is currently associated with PhillipCapital India in their portfolio-management services fund-management team, giving him a ringside view of the investing profession. He is a marathon runner and weightlifter, and has been doing both for the last fifteen years. He has also contributed articles to financial-services publications, appeared on podcasts and written blogs for health-tech startups and brands. He writes a personal blog on investing, health and psychology, and how these disciplines converge.

Mihir Patki is an investment professional with a deep passion for personal finance and nutrition. He started his career at Deloitte before transitioning to various capital markets roles with Bank of America Merrill Lynch and JM Financial. From 2013 to 2020, Mihir led CVK Advisors, a boutique advisory firm where he focused on special situations credit. In 2020, he co-founded Multipie, a social network for investors that grew into a vibrant community of over 1 lakh members from novices to seasoned experts. Multipie was acquired by ICICI Securities in 2022. Mihir currently works with Tata Capital's structured finance team. He is a chartered accountant and holds an MBA from the University of Oxford.

HarperCollins *Publishers* India

At HarperCollins India, we believe in telling the best stories and finding the widest readership for our books in every format possible. We started publishing in 1992; a great deal has changed since then, but what has remained constant is the passion with which our authors write their books, the love with which readers receive them, and the sheer joy and excitement that we as publishers feel in being a part of the publishing process.

Over the years, we've had the pleasure of publishing some of the finest writing from the subcontinent and around the world, including several award-winning titles and some of the biggest bestsellers in India's publishing history. But nothing has meant more to us than the fact that millions of people have read the books we published, and that somewhere, a book of ours might have made a difference.

As we look to the future, we go back to that one word— a word which has been a driving force for us all these years.

Read.